Highlights

ULTIMATE PUZZLE CHALLENGE!

HIGHLIGHTS PRESS

Honesdale, Pennsylvania

CONTENTS

HIDDEN PICTURES® PUZZLES

CONTENTS

Word Play

Word Search

PICTURE PUZZLES

Check . . . and Double Check

Hidden in Plain Sight

Hidden Pieces

CONTENTS

MATH & LOGIC PUZZLES

ABOVE AND BEYOND— AND SUPER FUN!

SIZE UP State of Mind

These states look about the same size here, but they're actually very different. Can you put them in size order? Put a 1 next to the smallest state and a 6 next to the biggest.

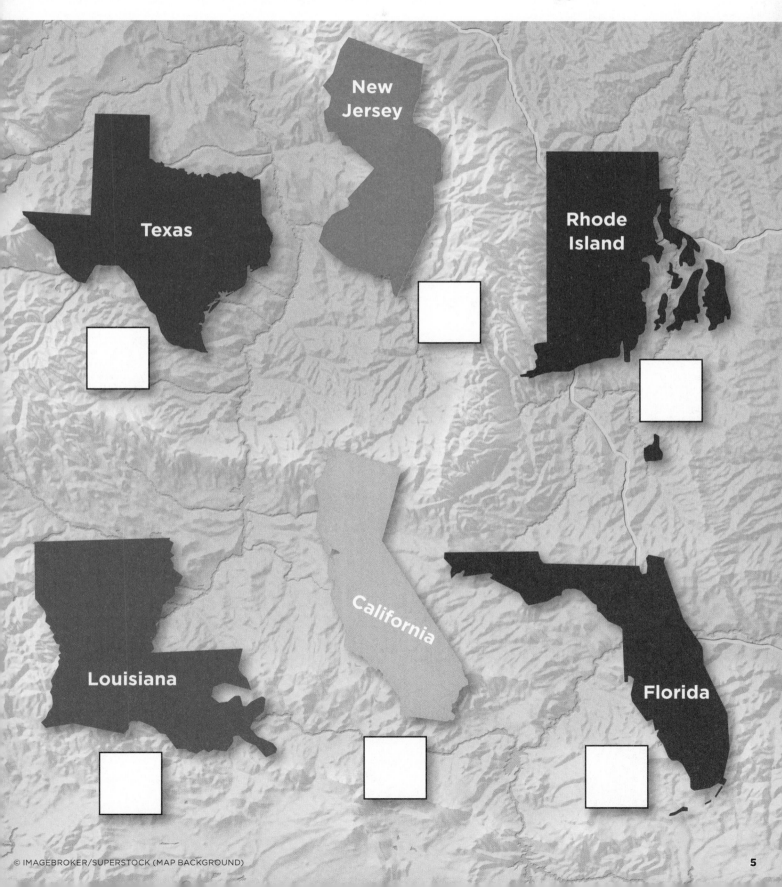

New Jersey

Texas

Rhode Island

Louisiana

California

Florida

Sizzling Summer Maze

You just bought some ice-cream cones. Can you get to your umbrella on the beach before they melt? Begin at START and make your way around sunbathers, towels, coolers, and sandcastles to your towel at the END.

Hidden Pictures® SUPER CHALLENGE

Chow Hounds

Hot dogs are on the menu—again! While these canines chow down, can you track down all **26 hidden objects**?

 artist's brush

 belt

 book

 coat hanger

 comb

 cupcake

 envelope

 flashlight

 flyswatter

 kite

 lollipop

 magnet

 paper airplane

 pencil

 rake

 ring

 ruler

 sailboat

 saw

 shoe

 sock

 stamp

 suitcase

 taco

 wedge of cheese

 wristwatch

8

ART BY KELLY KENNEDY

Brave New Crisscross

The list below has 32 words that can mean *brave*. They fit in the grid in only one way. Use the number of letters in each word as a clue to where it might fit. We started you off with *BOLD*.

4 LETTERS

BOLD

GAME

5 LETTERS

NERVY

NOBLE

6 LETTERS

CHEEKY

DARING

GRITTY

HEROIC

PLUCKY

SPUNKY

7 LETTERS

DASHING

DEFIANT

VALIANT

8 LETTERS

FEARLESS

INTREPID

RESOLUTE

SPIRITED

UNAFRAID

9 LETTERS

AUDACIOUS

CONFIDENT

DAUNTLESS

STEADFAST

TENACIOUS

10 LETTERS

COURAGEOUS

DETERMINED

HEADSTRONG

PERSISTENT

11 LETTERS

ADVENTUROUS

INDOMITABLE

LIONHEARTED

UNFLINCHING

12 LETTERS

HIGH-SPIRITED

BOLD

Monster Movie

You may or may not want to see the movie these creatures are watching, but you do have to keep your eyes open to find the **25 differences** between the two pages.

ART BY DARYLL COLLINS

Dog City

Quick! Study this page for one minute. Then turn to page 16 to test your memory!

ART BY NEIL NUMBERMAN

What's the Word?

Ten words have fallen to pieces—literally. Use the clues below to put the pieces back together. Each clue tells you the number of letters in that word. Cross the pieces off the list as you fill in the answers. Each piece can be used only once. We did one to get you started.

TIP:

Some pieces may work for more than one word, but there's only one combination that forms all 10 words.

WORD PIECES

VOL	XE	SUB	DO
SPE	PH	~~RE~~	MAR
KETB	ALL	ENT	TU
~~VA~~	MOM	LL	THER
BAS	ETER	CANO	IN
DI	BAN	ELE	ANA
~~MPL~~	SUND	SAS	CONT
INE	ANT	AE	TER

1. Count Dracula is this kind of monster (7 letters) __VAMPIRE__

2. Dessert made of ice cream, hot fudge, whipped cream, and a cherry on top (6 letters) _____

3. Device used to measure temperature (11 letters) _____

4. Europe, Africa, or North America, for example (9 letters) _____

5. Fancy suit worn at a wedding (6 letters) _____

6. Lava may erupt from it (7 letters) _____

7. Underwater vessel or big sandwich (9 letters) _____

8. Sport with hoops and nets (10 letters) _____

9. Largest living land animal (8 letters) _____

10. Yellow fruit loved by monkeys (6 letters) _____

FINISH THE JOKE:

When you're done, write the five unused pieces on the blanks to get the answer to this joke. Start at the top and go from left to right.

If you leave alphabet soup on the stove unattended, it could

___ ___ ___ ___ ___

___ ___ ___ ___ ___ ___ ___ ___ ___.

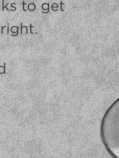

TEST YOUR MEMORY

Did you study the scene on page 14? Now see if you can answer these questions. Circle your responses. No peeking!

1. How many cats are taking pictures?

   2　　3　　1

2. Which one of these items is NOT on page 14?

   LEASH　　BOW TIE　　BONE

3. What is the correct color of this dog's shirt?

4. How many dogs are leaning out of car windows?

   2　　3　　4

5. There's a puzzle piece hidden on page 14. Where is it?

   ON A BUILDING
   ON A TAXI
   ON THE SIDEWALK

No Horsin'

Take a ride on this horsey word search and lasso the 27 words or phrases containing *HORSE* in the grid. The word *HORSE* has been replaced with 🐎. Look up, down, across, backward, and diagonally. The uncircled letters answer the riddle below.

WORD LIST

CLOTHESHORSE	PACKHORSE
DARK HORSE	RACE HORSE
EAT LIKE A HORSE	ROCKING HORSE
HOBBYHORSE	SAWHORSE
HOLD YOUR HORSES	SEA HORSE
HORSEBACK	STRONG AS A HORSE
HORSEFLY	TROJAN HORSE
HORSEHAIR	WARHORSE
HORSELAUGH	WORKHORSE
HORSEMANSHIP	
HORSEPLAY	
HORSEPOWER	
HORSE RACE	
HORSERADISH	
HORSESHOE	
HORSETAIL	
HORSEWHIP	
ONE HORSE TOWN	

Around

RIDDLE: **Why did the pony have to gargle? Put the uncircled letters in order on the blanks.**

ANSWER:

__ __ __ __ __ __ __ __ __ __

__ __ __ __ __ __ __ __ __ __ __ __ __.

Camping Out

Each of these scenes contains **12 hidden objects**, which are listed at the right. Find each object in one of the scenes, then cross it off the list.

Each object is hidden only once. Can you find them all?

banana
canoe
comb
cupcake
doughnut

envelope
fish
flowerpot
hammer
hot dog

ice-cream cone
ice skate
key
light bulb
mitten

pencil
pennant
slice of pizza
tape dispenser
telescope

toothbrush
waffle
wedge of cheese
yo-yo

Picture THIS

The words in each box show a common phrase. Pay attention to how the words are arranged to figure out the phrase. For example, in the first one, the word *SWIMMING* is under the word *WATER*. So the answer is *SWIMMING UNDERWATER*. Can you get them all?

1

ANSWER: SWIMMING UNDERWATER

2

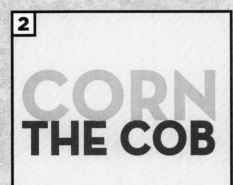

ANSWER:

3

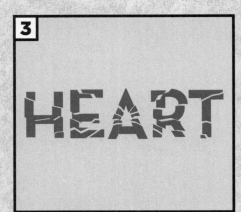

ANSWER:

4

ANSWER:

5

ANSWER:

6

ANSWER:

BRAIN SQUEEZE

Use these tricky questions to stump your family and friends.

1 I am an odd number. If you take away one of my letters, I become even. What number am I?

2 A cowboy rides in on Friday, stays for three days, and leaves on Friday. How did he do that?

Hidden in Plain Sight

Can you find the **16 cereal bowls** hidden in this photo?

ART BY BILL GOLLIHER; PHOTO BY PAMELA D. MCADAMS/ISTOCK

Let It Slide

The two kids in the START pool are each about to choose a different slide to start their trek to the FINISH pool . . . but which slide should each kid take? And when they make it to their first pool, which slide should they take then? That's your job to figure out!

Here are the lifeguard's rules for enjoying the waterslide:

- You must travel from top to bottom on slides. No climbing or swimming up the slides.
- You can't use the same pools or slides as the other slide rider. No sharing slides!

HINT: There is only one route from the top to the bottom for each kid. Good luck!

START

FINISH

MAZE CREATED AND ILLUSTRATED BY ROBERT PRINCE

HINKS PINKS

Read each clue below. The answers are Hinks Pinks, pairs of words that rhyme. We did one to get you started.

HINK PINK:
Each answer is a pair of one-syllable rhyming words.

1. Shore talk:
   ___BEACH___ ___SPEECH___

2. Drab choo-choo:
   _____ _____

HINKY PINKY:
Each answer is a pair of two-syllable rhyming words.

3. Chillier rock: _____ _____

4. Arctic tooth: _____ _____

HINKETY PINKETY:
The answer is a pair of three-syllable rhyming words.

5. The White House: _____ _____

BONUS ROUND:

1. **Hink Pink:** Steak stealer:
   _____ _____

2. **Hinky Pinky:** Lawyer dog:
   _____ _____

3. **Hinkety Pinkety:** Flavored ape:
   _____ _____

Go for a Spin

Use the clues below to fill in the boxes of this spiral—**but there's a twist:** the last letter of each word is also the first letter of the next word. Use the linking letters to help you spin all the way to the center. We did the first one for you.

1. Activity in which you slide down a snowy hill
8. These keep your hands warm.
13. An ice crystal that falls from the sky in winter
21. Santa's helpers
25. Wrap this around your neck to stay warm.
29. Water _____ at 32° Fahrenheit.
35. What you get when snow and ice start to melt
39. Warm chocolaty drink (2 words)
46. Where you find the South Pole
55. Where you find the North Pole
60. Heavy outer article of clothing
63. These may chatter when you're cold.
67. Warms
71. You can build this "guy" outside after a winter storm.
77. Cold toes sometimes feel this way.
80. What winds do
83. Coldest season of the year
88. Where you ice-skate or play hockey
91. Makes hats out of wool
95. Season that marks the end of cold weather

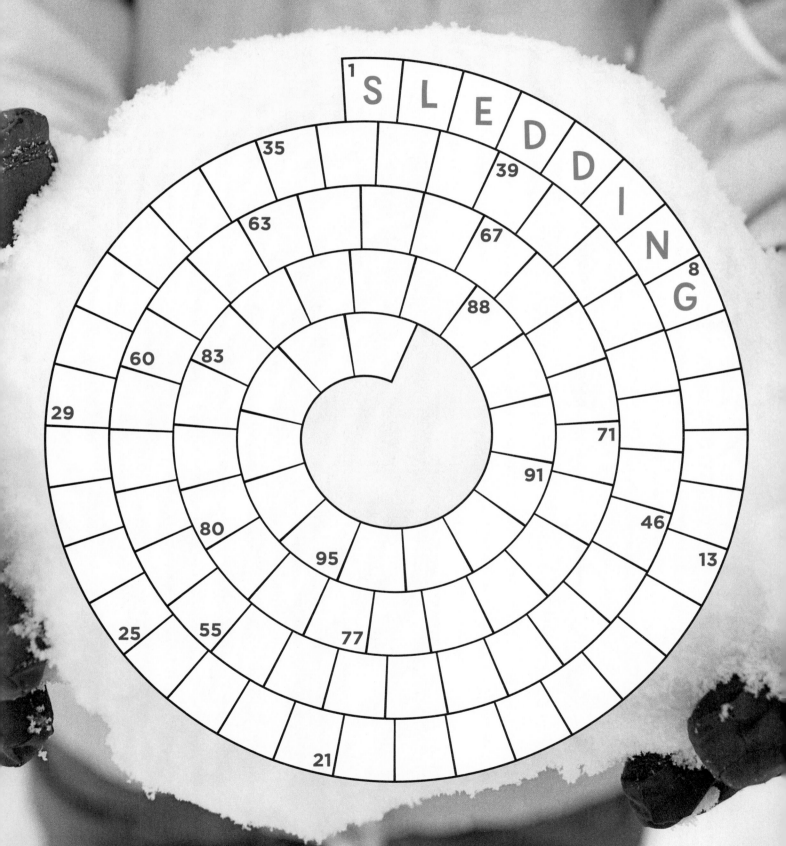

ZEBRA ZONE

There is more than meets the eye in this photo. Focus in, and see if you can find all **24 objects** hiding here.

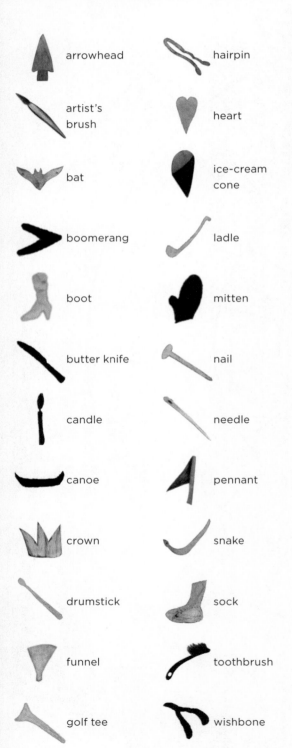

- arrowhead
- artist's brush
- bat
- boomerang
- boot
- butter knife
- candle
- canoe
- crown
- drumstick
- funnel
- golf tee
- hairpin
- heart
- ice-cream cone
- ladle
- mitten
- nail
- needle
- pennant
- snake
- sock
- toothbrush
- wishbone

Keep on Truckin'

Grab a bite and find the **25 differences** between these two pages.

ART BY DAVID COULSON

♦ Hidden Pieces ♦

UP, UP, AND AWAY!

Can you find these **11 jigsaw pieces** in this photo of hot-air balloons?

The Legion OF Super Solvers™

This super trio (from left, the Gentleman Gorilla™, Count Yoga™, and the Human Turnip™) uses puzzle powers to keep the world safe from wrong answers.

THE MAJOR MELTDOWN MYSTERY

Oh, no—puzzles are in peril! A short-tempered member of the villain society PFFT—Puzzle Fiends Fighting Together—is tired of getting the wrong answers and has been taking out her frustration on puzzle pages everywhere. But the villain left behind three puzzles that will reveal her name. Can you solve the puzzles and capture the cranky scoundrel? Each puzzle will give you a key word. Use all three key words to catch the evil supervillain.

Moody Clues

The mystery villain is so angry, she is tearing words in half! Can you piece together the five words that are synonymous with *angry* or *crabby*? When you're done, you'll be left with two unused halves. Combine those to make your key word.

> WORDS CANNOT DESCRIBE THIS VILLAIN'S BEHAVIOR. WELL, THEY CAN, BUT FIRST YOU HAVE TO HELP ME PUT THEM BACK TOGETHER.

ATED	GROU	MPY
CHY	GRU	MU
CRA	IOUS	NKY
FUR	IRRIT	TANT

Write the leftover word.

KEY WORD: _____

The Gentleman Gorilla

32

Count Yoga

Stomping Ground

The mystery villain stomped on Count Yoga's favorite puzzle book and hid it at the end of this maze. Find the only path through the maze from START to FINISH. Then write down the letters you passed through in order. That's your key word.

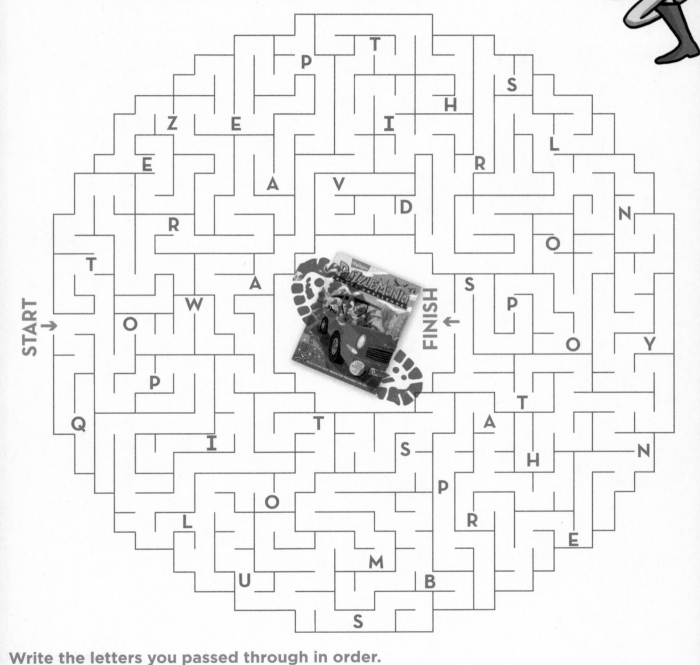

Write the letters you passed through in order.

KEY WORD: _____ _____ _____ _____ _____

Weed It and Reap

The mystery villain tossed a strange variety of items into the Human Turnip's garden. Follow the directions for crossing out items. You'll be left with one object. That's your key word.

HINT: The names of all the objects are three-letter words.

The Human Turnip

I LIKE A NICE TOSSED SALAD, BUT I DON'T LIKE VILLAINS TOSSING STUFF INTO MY GARDEN!

1. Cross out any pictures that rhyme with *FLY*.

2. Cross out any picture whose name ends in a double letter.

3. Cross out the two pictures whose names have their letters in reverse order of each other.

4. Cross out any picture whose name becomes a new word if you place the letter *B* in front.

5. Cross out any picture whose name becomes *PAN* if you change one letter.

6. Cross out the two pictures whose names become question words if you place the letter *W* in front.

Write the name of the only object that's left.

KEY WORD: _____ _____ _____

The Mystery Villain Revealed!

Place the key words in the blanks. Then copy each letter to the same numbered square below to catch the villain.

THE GENTLEMAN GORILLA'S KEY WORD:	COUNT YOGA'S KEY WORD:	THE HUMAN TURNIP'S KEY WORD:
__ __ __ __ __ __	__ __ __ __ __	__ __ __
14 13 4 2 7 11	3 9 6 10 8	1 5 12

THE VILLAIN IS:

| 1 | 2 | 3 | 4 | 5 | 6 | 7 | | 8 | 9 | 10 | 11 | 12 | 13 | 14 |

Now that you know the villain's name—
and all the whining and yelling has stopped—draw what she looks like here.

CAPTURED!

For the Birds

Each of these scenes contains **12 hidden objects**, which are listed at the right. Find each object in one of the scenes, then cross it off the list.

Each object is hidden only once. Can you find them all?

ax
bottle
~~bowling ball~~
button
cane

crayon
crescent moon
drinking straw
fish
flashlight

glove
harmonica
mallet
peanut
pineapple

radish
sailboat
shoe
slice of pie
tack

toothbrush
wedge of cheese
wedge of orange
yo-yo

These sudoku puzzles use letters instead of numbers. Fill in the squares so that the six letters appear only once in each row, column, and 2x3 box. Then read the yellow squares to find out the answer to the riddle.

LETTERS: A B I L R Z

	A			L	R
I		L		Z	B
Z			L		
	I	R			
	L				
R			B	A	

RIDDLE

- I am the only South American country whose official language is Portuguese.

- Thanks to the Amazon rain forest, I contain the most species of animals and plants in the world.

- I produce the most orange juice in the world.

  What country am I?

RIDDLE

- I am a colorless, odorless, and tasteless gas.

- I make up 21 percent of the air you breathe.

- I combine with two atoms of hydrogen to make water.

  What am I?

LETTERS: E G N X O Y

		G	E		
G					Y
N		G			E
X				N	Y
	N				X
			Y		

38

Monster Pets

The Fleezles™ are a typical family of monsters who love to star in logic puzzles!

Grand Fleezles   Sister   Brother   Dad   Mom

The Fleezles are playing fetch with their pets. Using the clues below and looking at the pictures of the pets, figure out which pet belongs to which Fleezle and which toy each pet is fetching. Put an *O* in each box that must be true in the chart and an *X* in each box that can't be true.

TIP: Fill in all three sections of the grid as you read the clues. It will help you solve the puzzle.

CLUES

1. The Grand Fleezles' pet has two tails and loves bones.

2. Spot refuses to fetch balls.

3. Russ and the pet that likes shoes have three-legged owners.

4. Mom likes to toss a flying disk to her pet with one of her many hands, but she's allergic to winged pets.

5. Brother and Sister aren't allowed pets that have spikes or horns or breathe fire.

	Puff	Russ	Spike	Spot	Tiny	Ball	Bone	Flying Disk	Shoe	Stuffed Animal
Mom										
Dad										
Sister										
Brother										
Grand Fleezles										
Ball										
Bone										
Flying Disk										
Shoe										
Stuffed Animal										

Tiny

Spot

Spike   Russ   Puff

Class Trek: Quarkle Middle School Visits Earth

D-Leader and the students in her out-of-this-world cultures class are on another field trip. This time, they left Planet Q to check out a ball game at Boston's Fenway Park. As usual, all the students got lost instantly. Can you help D-Leader find her **6 students** in the big scene? Then look for the items on their field-trip checklist. Check off each one you find.

Can you find my students in the crowd?

J-KUB   B-BOP   KAY-T   C-YAH   N-DROO   BUG-Z

FIELD-TRIP CHECKLIST

- 3 soft pretzels
- 1 pair of binoculars
- 1 green purse
- 6 ice-cream cones
- 1 green baseball cap
- 1 sleeping person
- the number 1918
- the number 33
- 3 pigeons
- 3 hot dogs
- 1 teddy bear
- 5 water bottles
- 1 person reading a book
- 4 tubs of popcorn
- 1 kid blowing a bubble
- 2 blue checked shirts

ART BY CHUCK DILLON

Hidden Pictures

6
by Six

Each of these small scenes contains 6 hidden objects from the list below. Some objects are hidden in more than one scene. Can you figure out which 6 objects are hidden in each scene?

HIDDEN OBJECT LIST

artist's brush (3)	paper clip (4)
baseball bat (3)	ring (2)
bell (4)	shoe (2)
domino (3)	spoon (2)
ice-cream cone (2)	tack (5)
lollipop (3)	toothbrush (3)

The numbers tell you how many times each object is hidden.

42

BONUS MATCH
Two scenes contain the exact same set of hidden objects. Can you find that matching pair?

ART BY NEIL NUMBERMAN

One Sweet Crisscross

When it's time for something sweet, what do you choose? This puzzle might help you decide. The 30 treats listed below fit in the grid in only one way. Use the number of letters in each sweet as a clue to where it might fit. We did one to get you started.

4 LETTERS

FLAN

5 LETTERS

APPLE

PEACH

6 LETTERS

COOKIE

GELATO

ICE POP

MUD PIE

SORBET

7 LETTERS

BAKLAVA

BLONDIE

BROWNIE

CANNOLI

CUPCAKE

8 LETTERS

ICE CREAM

MACAROON

PEAR TART

SMOOTHIE

TIRAMISU

9 LETTERS

CHERRY PIE

10 LETTERS

APPLE CRISP

CHEESECAKE

FRUIT SALAD

KEY LIME PIE

11 LETTERS

BLUEBERRIES

12 LETTERS

PEACH CRUMBLE

13 LETTERS

FORTUNE COOKIE

RED VELVET CAKE

SNICKERDOODLE

14 LETTERS

RAINBOW SHERBET

16 LETTERS

BLUEBERRY COBBLER

COOKIE

Snow Day

Quick! Study this page for one minute. Then turn to page 48 to test your memory!

Dance Marathon

Hidden Pictures®
SUPER CHALLENGE

Before you join the dance marathon, see if you can find the **38 hidden objects**.

FIND THESE OBJECTS: baby's bottle, banana, bell, book, boot, bowl, butterfly, can, caterpillar, clothespin, comb, cracker, cupcake, domino, eyeglasses, fan, fish, flashlight, funnel, glove, heart, hourglass, lamp, leaf, light bulb, lipstick tube, magnet, mushroom, peanut, pencil, pillow, ring, sailboat, saltshaker, saw, slice of bread, tack, and teacup.

ART BY DIANA ZOURELIAS

Did you study the scene on page 46? Now see if you can answer these questions. Circle your responses. No peeking!

1. How many buttons does the snowman have?

     3   2   1

2. Which of these is NOT on page 46?

SHOVEL   MITTENS   GLOVES

3. What is the correct color of this boy's hat?

4. How many knit hats are on page 46?

     5   4   3

5. There's a puzzle piece hidden on page 46. Where is it?

ON A HOUSE

IN A WINDOW

ON A SCARF

Take the Bait

There's something fishy about this puzzle. That's because there are 29 words containing *FISH* hidden in the grid. The word *FISH* has been replaced with 🐟 . Look up, down, across, backward, and diagonally, and circle each word.

WORD LIST

ANGELFISH	FLYING FISH
ARCHERFISH	GOLDFISH
BLOWFISH	JELLYFISH
BLUEFISH	KINGFISH
BONEFISH	NOODLE FISH
BUTTERFISH	PARROT FISH
CATFISH	RIBBONFISH
CRAYFISH	SCORPION FISH
CUTTLEFISH	SHELLFISH
DOGFISH	STARFISH
FISHBOWL	SUNFISH
FISHERMAN	SWORDFISH
FISH-EYE	TRIGGERFISH
FISHHOOK	ZEBRA FISH
FISHTAIL	

B U T T E R  A G O L D

O L E L T T U C L D N D

T I E P A R R O T O I R

F A R C H E R S I H O

L T M H A I R C P H L W

Y A V B E R R O E W S

I E N B G A O O N O T E U

N W O G Y C K O B E O U N

G N I S T B Y O E L

R D O G L E G N A B R

T T B L O W Y L L E J A

K I N G Z E B R A H T

S H E L L E L D O O N S

Match-Up↑ Dragons

Can you find the **4 pairs** of identical dragons, the **3 dragons** that are exactly alike, and the **1 dragon** that has no match?

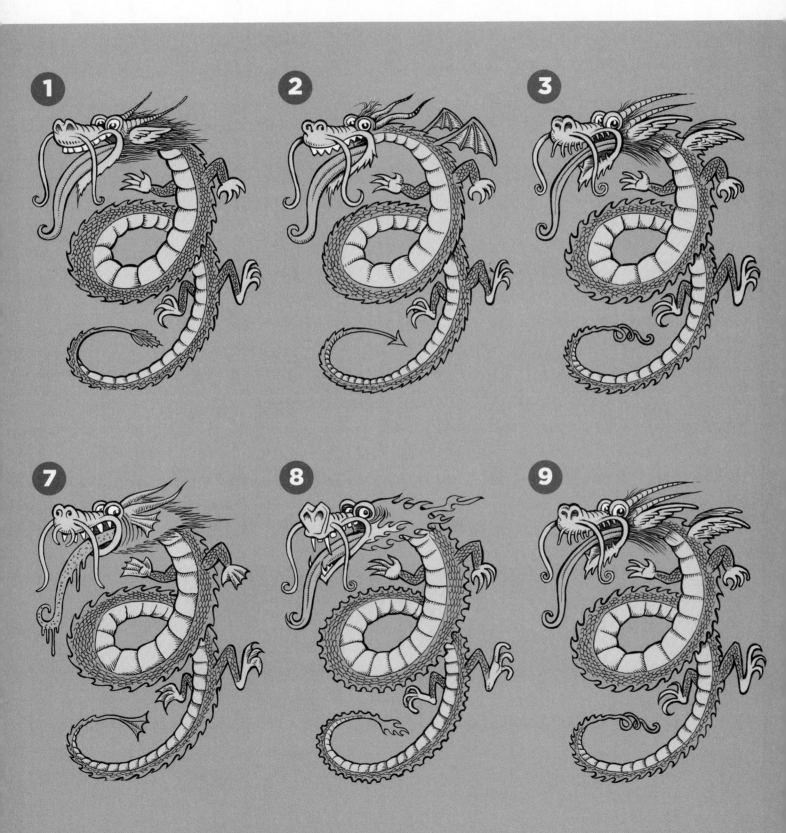

Fill in your answers here.

Pair: ___ and ___   Pair: ___ and ___

Pair: ___ and ___   Trio: ___, ___, and ___

Pair: ___ and ___   Single: ___

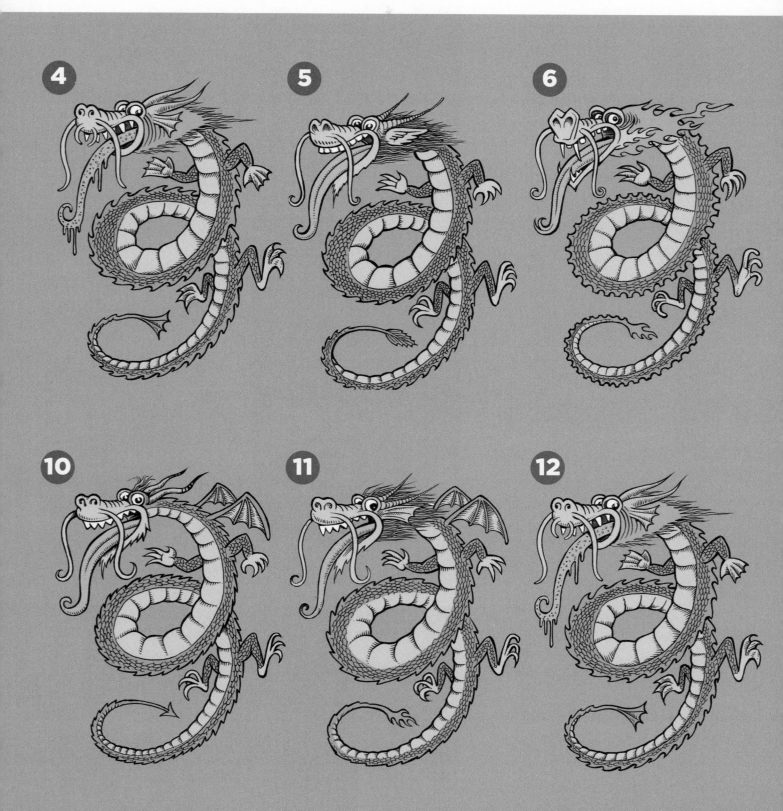

Hidden Pictures®
SUPER CHALLENGE

Carrot Craving

Carrots are always on the menu at Chez Carrot. While the customers crunch, you can dig in and find the **19 hidden objects**.

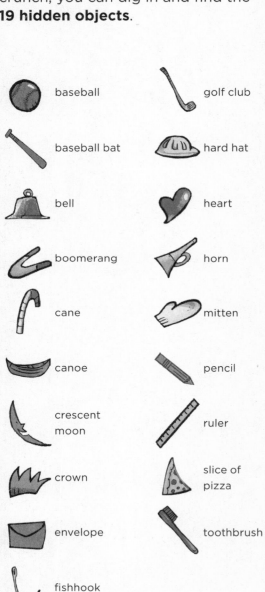

baseball

golf club

baseball bat

hard hat

bell

heart

boomerang

horn

cane

mitten

canoe

pencil

crescent moon

ruler

crown

slice of pizza

envelope

toothbrush

fishhook

BONUS SNACK: Can you find 5 peppermints in this scene?

NUMBER CRUNCH

> People, you know how to add, subtract, multiply, and divide, right? Then you can play calcudoku! Warm up with lunges, lots of them . . . *NOW!*

HOW TO PLAY:

- To complete a game, each number will appear only once in a row and only once in a column, like in sudoku.

- The set of squares inside the heavy lines is called a cage. Each cage shows a bold number and a math sign. The math sign (+, -, x, /) tells you to add, subtract, multiply, or divide.

- The cage's bold number is the answer to the equation. For example, "12x" means that the numbers in the cage's squares must equal 12 when they are multiplied.

HERE'S AN EXAMPLE:

The only possible numbers for **2/** in this puzzle are 2 and 1. You may not know which number goes where, so write the numbers down as possibilities in the corners of the squares.

It's good to start with the multiplication cages. 18x can only be 3x3x2. And just like in sudoku, you can't put the 3s in the same row or column (but they can be in the same cage).

Since the **2/** cage uses the numbers 2 and 1, the top square of the **4+** cage must be a 3.

An equal sign after a number means that you should put that number in the square.

The order of the numbers in a cage doesn't matter, but there's only one order that works in the finished puzzle.

2/ **1**	2	4+ **3**
18x **2**	3	1
3	1- **1**	2

CUTE 3x3 PUZZLE
(NUMBERS 1–3)

3=	2x	6+
1-		

FRIENDLY 4x4 PUZZLE
(NUMBERS 1–4)

10+		6x	
	3/		
9x	2-		7+

FIERCE 5x5 PUZZLE
(NUMBERS 1–5)

14+		2/		11+
2-		30x		
	9x			2-
			25x	
	2/			

WRITTEN BY ANDREW BRISMAN; ACE ART BY R. SIKORYAK;
PHOTO BY EMRAH TURUDU/EXACTOSTOCK/SUPERSTOCK (CHALKBOARD)

Class Trek: Quarkle Middle School Visits Earth

D-Leader and the students in her out-of-this-world cultures class are on another field trip. They've left Planet Q to visit the Louvre Museum in Paris, France. As usual, all the students got lost in a flash. Can you help D-Leader find her **6 students** in the big scene? Then look for the items on their field-trip checklist. Check off each one you find.

FIELD-TRIP CHECKLIST

- [ ] 1 guitar
- [ ] 4 dogs
- [ ] 2 balloons
- [ ] 1 green hooded sweatshirt

- [ ] 5 red backpacks
- [ ] 1 wheelchair
- [ ] 1 yellow flower
- [ ] 9 birds

- [ ] the number 3
- [ ] 1 taco
- [ ] 1 ice-cream cone
- [ ] 1 yellow headband

- [ ] the number 12
- [ ] 2 books
- [ ] 1 bow tie
- [ ] 1 blue barrette

ART BY CHUCK DILLON

Squish Squash

Squash is one of the oldest known crops. Some of the varieties are pictured here. Can you go from one end of the maze to the other? Begin at START and make your way to FINISH, passing through the numbers in order from 1 to 5 without backtracking or repeating any routes. Good luck!

START

ART AND MAZE BY ELIZABETH CARPENTER

Step Right Up!

It's a perfect day for the amusement park—and to find at least **25 differences** between these two pages.

COTTON CANDY

PIZZA

Monster Music School

The Fleezles™ are a typical family of monsters who love to star in logic puzzles!

Grand Fleezles   Sister   Brother   Dad   Mom

The Fleezles are meeting their music teachers for instrument lessons. Using the clues below and looking at the pictures of the teachers, figure out what instrument each Fleezle plays and with what teacher. Put an O in each box in the chart that must be true and an X in each box that can't be true.

TIP: Fill in all three sections of the chart as you read the clues. It will help you solve the puzzle.

Drakeula

CLUES

1. The music school doesn't allow more than four heads or six legs in a practice room.

2. Brother is using his extra fingers on a stringed instrument.

3. Katy Scary always reminds her student not to put all three feet on the piano pedals.

4. The guitar student and teacher both wear glasses.

5. Mom's drum teacher has one more eye than Dad's saxophone teacher.

	Drums	Guitar	Piano	Saxophone	Violin	Drakeula	Bruno From Mars	Lady GooGoo	Katy Scary	Three Directions
Mom										
Dad										
Sister										
Brother										
Grand Fleezles										
Drakeula										
Bruno From Mars										
Lady GooGoo										
Katy Scary										
Three Directions										

Three Directions

Lady GooGoo

Katy Scary

Bruno From Mars

Hidden in Plain Sight

Can you find the **12 bowling balls** hidden in this photo?

Rhymin' in the Rain

The downpour may be over, but there are **16** items in the picture below that rhyme with the word RAIN. Can you find them all?

ART BY JAMES YAMASAKI

Just Add WORDS

Match one picture with one word to make a compound word. The picture can go before or after the word. Some pictures may have more than a single match, but there is only one solution that creates 15 compound words. We started you off with SCARECROW.

scare

mint

place

back

under

pop

green

pick

sweet

blue

worm

sitter

hole

room

sun

1. <u>Scarecrow</u>

2. _____

3. _____

4. _____

5. _____

6. _____

7. _____

8. _____

9. _____

10. _____

11. _____

12. _____

13. _____

14. _____

15. _____

Lights, Camera, SEARCH!

Circle the 25 words about movies in this grid. Look up, down, across, backward, and diagonally. The uncircled letters answer the trivia question at the bottom.

WORD LIST

ACTION
ACTORS
ANIMATION
AWARDS
CAST
DRAMATIC
FAMOUS
FICTION
FILM
FUNNY
HOLLYWOOD
HORROR
LOBBY
MUSICAL
PLOT
POPCORN
PROPS
SCARY
SCRIPT
SLAPSTICK
SLOW MOTION
SOUNDTRACK
STAR
STUNTS
VILLAIN

```
S  T  H  L  N  O  I  T  A  M  I  N  A
C  S  A  S  O  U  N  D  T  R  A  C  K
R  L  T  T  P  B  N  R  O  C  P  O  P
I  A  S  D  S  O  B  S  T  U  N  T  S
P  P  L  O  P  A  R  Y  O  O  N  N  C
T  S  O  O  P  U  C  P  I  O  F  I  I
L  T  W  W  R  L  L  T  I  U  A  A  T
A  I  M  Y  A  O  C  T  N  R  L  L  A
C  C  O  L  T  A  C  N  S  F  I  L  M
I  K  T  L  S  I  Y  E  T  C  T  I  A
S  E  I  O  F  A  M  O  U  S  A  V  R
U  R  O  H  R  H  O  R  R  O  R  R  D
M  I  N  S  E  S  S  D  R  A  W  A  Y
```

TRIVIA QUESTION:

Which letter is used the most in English?
Put the uncircled letters in order on the blanks.

ANSWER:

___ ___ ___ ___   ___ ___ ___ ___ ___ ___ ___

___ ___ ___ ___ ___ ___   ___ ___   ___.

Day and Night

Each of these scenes contains **12 hidden objects**, which are listed at the right. Find each object in one of the scenes, then cross it off the list.

Each object is hidden only once. Can you find them all?

acorn
artist's brush
banana
baseball bat
button

candle
comb
crescent moon
cupcake
domino

doughnut
envelope
hockey stick
iron
ladder

mitten
pencil
popcorn
rolling pin
ruler

sailboat
thimble
toothbrush
waffle

♟ Hidden Pieces ❖
PENGUIN POSES

Can you find these **11 jigsaw pieces** in this photo of king penguins?

Sit, Stay, Solve

All kinds of animals make good pets. But only five of them fit in this puzzle. Fill in the correct answers, then think about what kind of pet you'd like to have. HINT: If you don't know the answer to a clue, look at the other clues that are around it, both across and down, or try another part of the puzzle and come back to the tough clue later.

ACROSS

1 Part of your foot that a nursery rhyme calls "a little piggy"

4 Abbreviation for tender loving care

7 Grain that's in a granola bar

8 Salsa or hummus, for example

11 What you hear with

12 Abbreviation for National Flute Association

13 Abbreviation for earned run average

14 Also known as; fake name

16 "The candles were ___ and the room looked spooky."

17 Household Pet #1: I'm furry with big ears.

19 Household Pet #2: I have scales.

20 Main girl in The Nutcracker; rhymes with Sara

22 Household Pet #3: I'm feathered.

25 Household Pet #4: I'm small, furry, and fast.

29 Number before two

30 Campfire treat made of chocolate, marshmallows, and graham crackers

31 " ___ a girl!" (birth announcement)

32 " ___ ___ dreaming?"; Is this really happening? (2 words)

34 Harry Potter's best male friend

35 Parking ___ (a place to leave cars)

36 Household Pet #5: I'm man's best friend.

37 "The ___" (closing words of a story)

38 Dad's boy

DOWN

1 One of a pair of glands in the throat that can get swollen when you're sick

2 Clumsy person

3 Abbreviation for estimated time of arrival

4 When you're sad, one might fall down your cheek

5 Sing tra-___-___ (2 words)

6 Baby's place to sleep

8 Short name for a shop that sells sliced meats and sandwiches

9 Colored part of the eye (also the name of a flower)

10 "Always stay on the marked ___ when you're in the woods."

15 First four letters of the alphabet

18 Chasing game in which one person is It

19 Old MacDonald had one.

21 Quit a job

22 Do this to water to cook spaghetti.

23 Get ___ shape

24 "I need some R&R: ___ and relaxation."

26 "That movie was such a ___. I kept falling asleep!"

27 Take wrinkles out of clothes.

28 Give temporarily

32 Commercials

33 Dairy farm sound

WRITTEN BY BRENDAN EMMETT QUIGLEY; PHOTOS BY CAIA IMAGES/SUPERSTOCK (ALL DOGS)

The Legion OF Super Solvers™

This super trio (from left, the Gentleman Gorilla™, Count Yoga™, and the Human Turnip™) uses puzzle powers to keep the world safe from wrong answers.

THE CASE OF THE PILFERED PILLOWS

After a busy day of puzzle solving, everyone deserves a good night's rest. But a member of the villain society PFFT—Puzzle Fiends Fighting Together—has stolen the world's pillow supply! The sleep-robbing thief left behind three puzzles that reveal his name. Can you solve the puzzles and nab the crook? Each puzzle will give you a key word. Use all three key words to catch the evil supervillain.

Hidden Nature

Find each animal word in the grid below by moving from square to square—in any direction. You can use the same square in more than one word, but never more than once in the same word. (We did one for you.) Then write the unused letters, from left to right and top to bottom, to reveal one more hidden animal. That's your key word.

Find These Animals:

BEAR ELEPHANT ~~LION~~ TIGER ZEBRA

I	R	N	T	E
L	O	I	A	L
H	G	H	P	E
I	E	R	E	B
Z	B	N	A	O

THEY MAY NOT BE SNAPPY DRESSERS, BUT THEY'RE SOME OF MY *BEAST* FRIENDS.

The Gentleman Gorilla

Write the unused letters in order.

KEY WORD: ____ ____ ____ ____ ____ ____ ____

Teddy, Set, Go!

The mystery villain not only poached Count Yoga's pillow, he hid the count's teddy bear at the end of this maze. Find the only path through the maze from START to FINISH. Then write down the letters you passed through in order. That's your key word.

WHAT KIND OF TWISTED MIND TAKES A MAN'S TEDDY BEAR?

Count Yoga

START

FINISH

Write the letters you passed through in order.

KEY WORD: ___ ___ ___ ___ ___ ___ ___

WRITTEN BY ANDREW BRISMAN; ART BY R. SIKORYAK; PHOTO BY PICSFIVE/ISTOCK

R U Ready?

The answer to each clue below is a combination of a letter plus a pictured object. Say both the letters and pictures out loud to figure out the words. For example, the answer for the first clue is OCEAN, using the O and the pictured SHIN. After you answer all the clues, there will be one letter and pictured object left over. That's your key word.

The Human Turnip

THIS PUZZLE WAS STARTING TO MAKE MY *GREENS* WILT. THANKS FOR THE ASSIST!

P +

O +

N +

C +

B + **4**

A +

D +

G +

L +

1. The Atlantic or Pacific, for example

2. A kind of nut that's sometimes used to make pie.

3. You need it to keep the other team from scoring.

4. An oak tree can grow from it.

5. You may find it in a playground.

6. A magical creature often found in a lamp

7. The opposite of after

8. Where your arm bends.

Write the word made by the leftover letter and pictured object.

KEY WORD: _____ _____ _____ _____ _____ _____

The Mystery Villain Revealed!

Place the key words in the blanks. Then copy each letter to the same numbered square below to catch the villain.

THE GENTLEMAN GORILLA'S KEY WORD:

___ ___ ___ ___ ___
11 2 7 6 14

COUNT YOGA'S KEY WORD:

___ ___ ___ ___ ___ ___
8 1 15 10 4 12

THE HUMAN TURNIP'S KEY WORD:

___ ___ ___ ___ ___ ___
3 13 9 5 17 16

THE VILLAIN IS:

1	2	3		4	5	6	7	8	9	10	11		12	13	14	15	16	17

Everyone can rest easy again! Now that you know the villain's name, draw what he looks like here. (You may want to put in some earplugs first.)

CAPTURED!

Hidden Pictures®

6 by Six

Each of these small scenes contains **6 hidden objects** from the list below. Some objects are hidden in more than one scene. Can you find the 6 hidden objects in each scene?

HIDDEN OBJECT LIST

banana **(4)**	mitten **(4)**
broccoli **(2)**	mug **(2)**
clothespin **(2)**	saucepan **(2)**
cotton swab **(4)**	slice of pizza **(3)**
domino **(3)**	spatula **(3)**
drumstick **(4)**	wedge of orange **(3)**

The numbers tell you how many times each object is hidden.

ART BY NEIL NUMBERMAN

Spot the Bad Bots

At the Bizmo Brickbot factory, brickbots are created from the set of bricks shown below. However, **6** of the brickbots shown here cannot be built from only these bricks. Can you figure out which bots are the real deal and which bots are not?

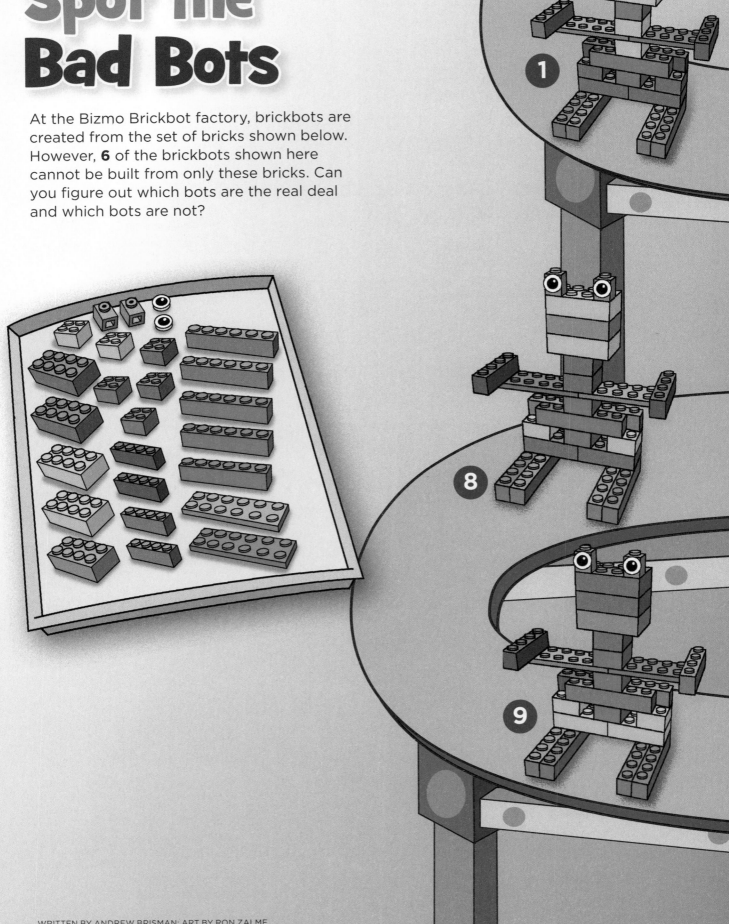

WRITTEN BY ANDREW BRISMAN; ART BY RON ZALME

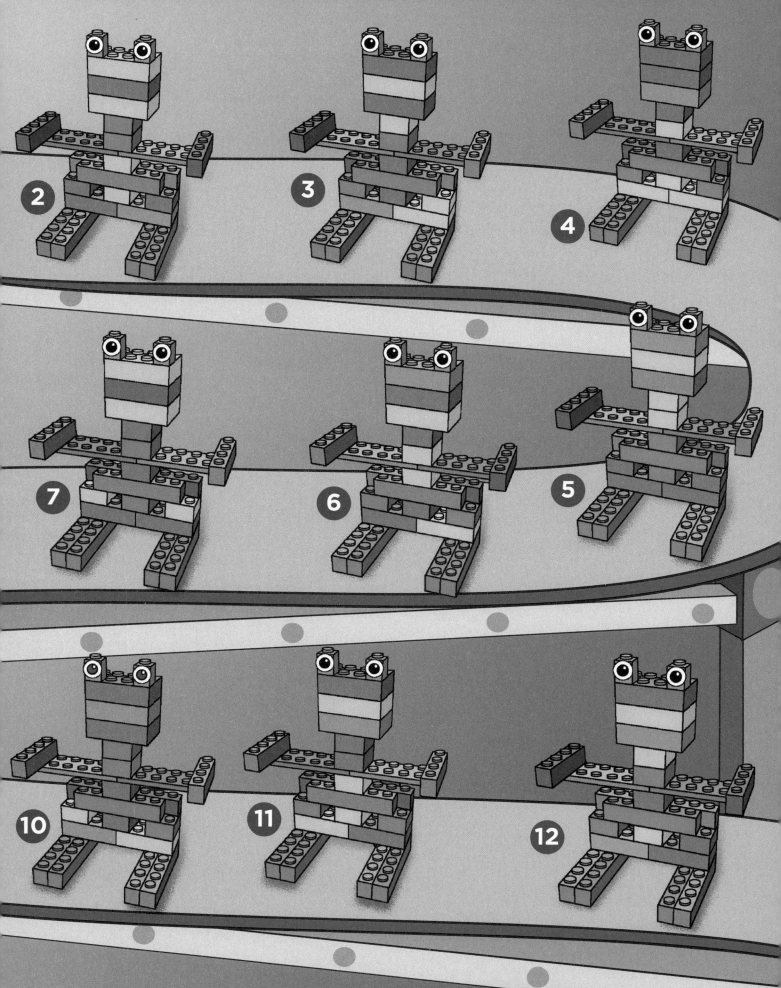

UNDER THE SEA

There is more than meets the eye in this photo. Focus in, and see if you can find all **16 objects** hiding here.

apple

barbell

bird

butterfly

Christmas tree

closed umbrella

comb

crescent moon

flag

glove

ice-cream cone

paintbrush

sailboat

shoe

slice of bread

wedge of lemon

Splash!

Don't get wet while doing this puzzle. Find the **25 differences** between these two pages.

WILD WAVE!

Est. 2002

NUMBER CRUNCH

People, you know how to add, subtract, multiply, and divide, right? Then you can play calcudoku! Now give me 30 jumping jacks on the page. I said *NOW!*

HOW TO PLAY:

- To complete a game, each number will appear only once in a row and only once in a column, like in sudoku.

- The set of squares inside the heavy lines is called a cage. Each cage shows a bold number and a math sign. The math sign (+, -, x, /) tells you to add, subtract, multiply, or divide.

- The cage's bold number is the answer to the equation. For example, "12x" means that the numbers in the cage's squares must equal 12 when they are multiplied.

HERE'S AN EXAMPLE:

The only possible numbers for 2/ in this puzzle are 2 and 1. You may not know which number goes where, so write the numbers down as possibilities in the corners of the squares.

It's good to start with the multiplication cages. 18x can only be 3x3x2. And just like in sudoku, you can't put the 3s in the same row or column (but they can be in the same cage).

Since the 2/ cage uses the numbers 2 and 1, the top square of the 4+ cage must be a 3.

2/ 1	2	4+ 3
18x 2	3	1
3	1- 1	2

An equal sign after a number means that you should put that number in the square.

The order of the numbers in a cage doesn't matter, but there's only one order that works in the finished puzzle.

CUTE 3x3 PUZZLE
(NUMBERS 1-3)

3x	1-	2=
		3/
5+		

FRIENDLY 4x4 PUZZLE
(NUMBERS 1-4)

3-		7+	3=
6x			
6+		1-	
4=		2/	

FIERCE 5x5 PUZZLE
(NUMBERS 1-5)

64x	2-		2/	
		4+		5x
5=		12x		
4-		4=	9+	
3/		3-		

WRITTEN BY ANDREW BRISMAN; ACE ART BY R. SIKORYAK;
PHOTO BY EMRAH TURUDU/EXACTOSTOCK/SUPERSTOCK (CHALKBOARD)

Funny Business

It's time for the annual meeting of Practical Jokers—and you're invited! Use the clues below to figure out the words. Each word is a hidden object to look for in the big scene. Once you've found the **13 hidden objects**, then transfer the letters with numbers into the correct spaces to learn the punch line to the joke.

1 Use this to row a boat.

<u>O</u> <u>A</u> <u>R</u>
1

2 This helps to hold up a pair of pants.

___ ___ ___ ___
2

3 Hammer and _____

___ ___ ___
3

4 Put this on before your shoe.

___ ___ ___
4

5 A toy that moves up and down on a string

___ ___ - ___ ___
5

6 Red Delicious or Granny Smith

___ ___ ___ ___ ___
6

7 The shape of a Valentine

___ ___ ___ ___ ___
7

8 Fork, knife, and _____

___ ___ ___ ___ ___
8

9 Use this to hit a ball off of a tee.

___ ___ ___ ___ ___   ___ ___ ___ ___
9

10 A toadstool

___ ___ ___ ___ ___ ___ ___
10

11 Clean your teeth with these bristles.

___ ___ ___ ___ ___ ___ ___ ___ ___ ___
11

12 Roll this down an alley toward pins.

___ ___ ___ ___ ___ ___ ___   ___ ___ ___ ___
12

13 This green plant is considered good luck.

___ ___ ___ ___ ___ - ___ ___ ___ ___ ___
13

___ ___ ___ ___ ___ ___

What is the difference between a rabbit that runs three miles a day and a so-so comedian?

<u>O</u> ___ ___   ___ ___   ___   ___ ___ ___
1 8 6   12 4   3   9 12 7

___ ___ ___ ___ ___ ;   ___ ___ ___
2 10 8 8 5   7 11 6

<u>O</u> ___ ___ ___ ___   ___ ___   ___
1 7 11 6 13   12 4   3

___ ___ ___   ___ ___ ___ ___ ___ .
2 12 7   9 10 8 8 5

Merry Crisscross!

When you finish this puzzle, you should be very happy. That's because the 31 words and phrases below are different ways to say *feeling happy*. They fit in the grid in only one way. Use the number of letters in each word or phrase as a clue to where it might fit. We did one to get you started.

5 LETTERS

HAPPY

JOLLY

~~MERRY~~

SUNNY

6 LETTERS

BLITHE

ELATED

JOYFUL

JOYOUS

UPBEAT

7 LETTERS

BEAMING

CHUFFED

GLEEFUL

JOCULAR

PLEASED

RADIANT

SMILING

8 LETTERS

BLISSFUL

CAREFREE

ECSTATIC

GRINNING

JUBILANT

THRILLED

9 LETTERS

ALL SMILES

CONTENTED

DELIGHTED

OVERJOYED

SATISFIED

11 LETTERS

EXHILARATED

12 LETTERS

LIGHTHEARTED

13 LETTERS

FLOATING ON AIR

IN GOOD SPIRITS

MERRY

Class Trek: Quarkle Middle School Visits Earth

D-Leader and the students in her out-of-this-world cultures class are on another field trip. They've left Planet Q to visit the Trevi Fountain in Rome, Italy. As usual, all the students got lost in a flash. Can you help D-Leader find her **6 students** in the big scene? Then look for the items on their field-trip checklist. Check off each one you find.

Can you find my students in the crowd?

J-KUB B-BOP KAY-T C-YAH N-DROO BUG-Z

FIELD-TRIP CHECKLIST

- 3 red backpacks
- 1 pinwheel
- 1 green-white-and-red striped hat
- 4 ice-cream cones
- 2 dogs
- 2 water bottles
- 1 stuffed animal
- 3 books
- 9 pairs of sunglasses
- 6 pigeons
- 1 closed umbrella
- 1 accordion
- 1 pair of crutches
- 4 phones
- 1 slice of pizza
- The word *ciao*

ART BY CHUCK DILLON

☷ Hidden Pieces ☷
FLOWER FUN

Can you find these **11 jigsaw pieces** in this photo of flowers?

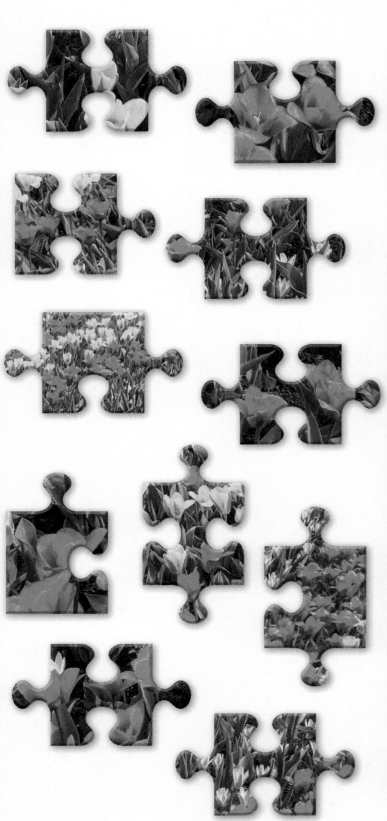

Hidden Pictures®
SUPER CHALLENGE

'Gator Skaters

Welcome to the Secret Society of 'Gator Skaters. You can join by searching for the **22 hidden objects** in this scene.

- apple
- bell
- cactus
- candy cane
- canoe
- dog bone
- Easter egg
- eyeglasses
- fish
- funnel
- horseshoe
- ice-cream bar
- ladle
- ruler
- skateboard
- slice of bread
- slice of pie
- slice of pizza
- snake
- teacup
- teapot
- three-leaf clover

BONUS SKATE: Can you find 5 lost mittens in this scene?

Match-Up
Hot-Air Balloons

Can you find the **4 pairs** of identical balloons, the **3 balloons** that are exactly alike, and the **1 balloon** that has no match?

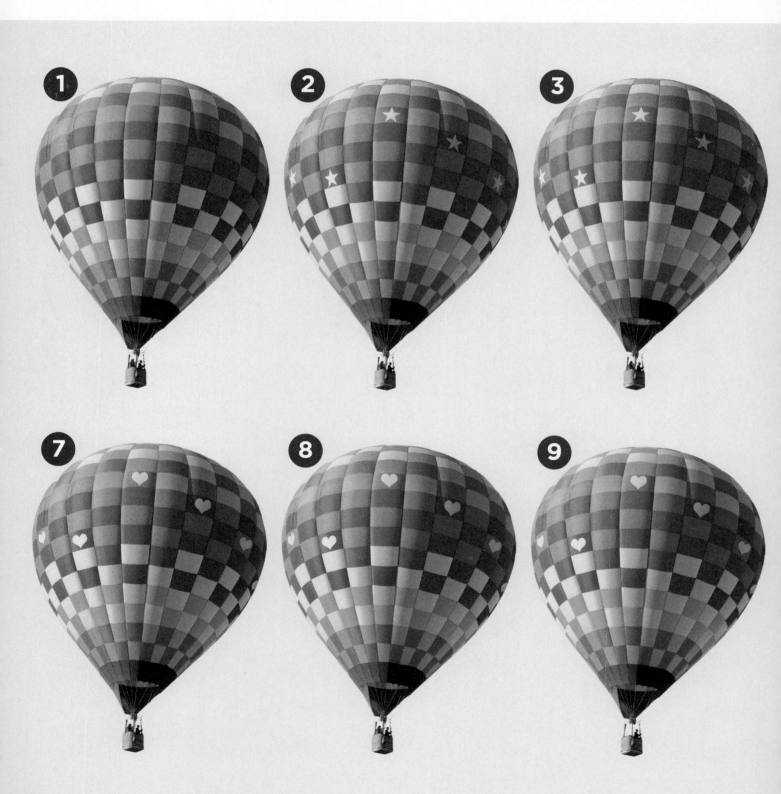

Fill in your answers here.

Pair: ___ and ___   Pair: ___ and ___

Pair: ___ and ___   Trio: ___, ___, and ___

Pair: ___ and ___   Single: ___

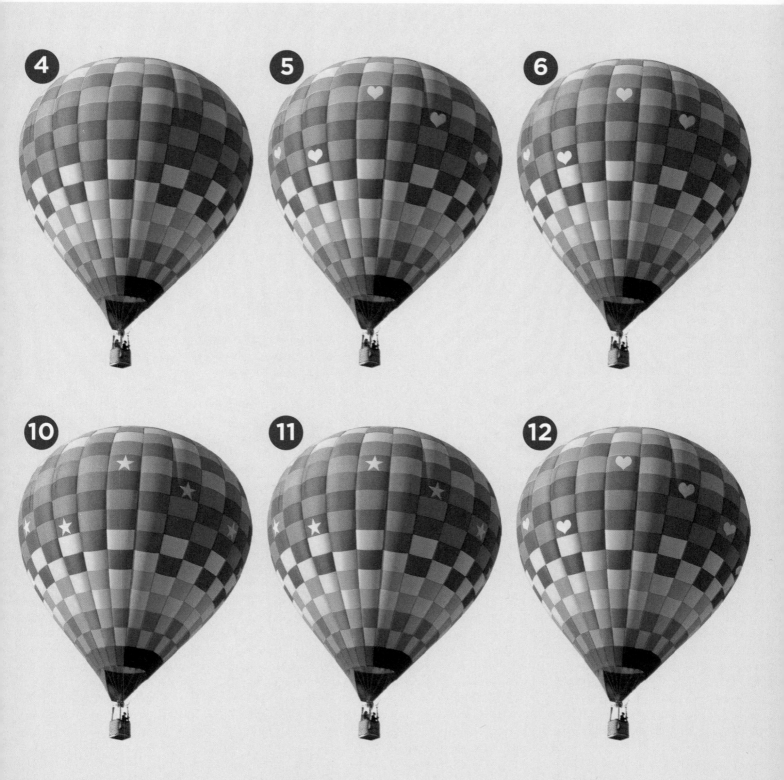

Zebra Crossing

No two zebras have the same set of stripes. Can you get through these zebras' unique stripes from START to FINISH? Go through the numbers in order from 1 to 5 without backtracking or repeating any routes. Good luck!

START

➜ **FINISH**

Underwater Yoga

Quick! Study this page for one minute. Then turn to page 104 to test your memory!

Picture THIS

The words in each box show a common phrase. Pay attention to how the words are arranged to figure out the phrase. For example, in the first one, the word *MIND* is over the word *MATTER*. So the answer is *MIND OVER MATTER*. Can you get them all?

1

ANSWER: MIND OVER MATTER

2

MY CENTS put CENTS

ANSWER:

3

choice CHOICE choice
choice choice choice
CHOICE choice choice
choice CHOICE choice

ANSWER:

4

ANSWER:

5

CHAIR

ANSWER:

6

tickled

ANSWER:

BRAIN SQUEEZE

Use these tricky questions to stump your family and friends.

1 A man was outside when it started to rain. He didn't have an umbrella and wasn't wearing a hat. Even though he was soaked, not a single hair on his head got wet. How could this happen?

2 What kind of room can no one enter?

TEST YOUR MEMORY

Did you study the scene on page 102? Now see if you can answer these questions. Circle your responses. No peeking!

1. How many yoga students does the octopus have?

    5   6   7

2. What is the correct color of the starfish?

3. What is the clam doing?

    STRETCHING   TWISTING
    STAYING SHUT

4. What creature is closest to the instructor?

    EEL   LOBSTER   CLAM

5. There's a puzzle piece hidden on page 102. Where is it?

    BETWEEN TWO FISH
    IN PURPLE CORAL
    ON THE SEA FLOOR

Where the ♥ Is

Follow your heart to do this puzzle. Circle the 24 words and phrases containing *HEART* hidden in this grid. The word *HEART* has been replaced with ♥. Look up, down, across, backward, and diagonally. The uncircled letters answer the heartfelt question below.

WORD LIST

BROKENHEARTED	**HEARTFELT**
CHANGE OF HEART	**HEART OF GOLD**
CHICKENHEARTED	**HEART OF STONE**
COLDHEARTED	**HEARTSICK**
HALF-HEARTED	**HEARTTHROB**
HARD-HEARTED	**HEART TO HEART**
HAVE A HEART	**HEARTWORM**
HEARTACHE	**KINDHEARTED**
HEART AND SOUL	**KNOW BY HEART**
HEARTBEAT	**SWEETHEART**
HEARTBREAK	**TENDERHEARTED**
HEARTBURN	**YOUNG AT HEART**

♥ O F G O L D E H C A ♥ ♥
E N O T S F O ♥ Y O U T R
D E ♥ N E K O R B T E A H
K C H I C K E N ♥ E D G E
I H ♥ T H R O B W N A N ♥
N A M B A R R S ♥ D D U F
D R R T U E H Y I E E O O
♥ D O K A R B A S R ♥ Y E
E ♥ W K C W N ♥ V ♥ F O G
D E ♥ ♥ O I N ♥ F E L T N
E D T N G I S A N D A T A
P O K C O L D ♥ E D H ♥ H
♥ U M P ♥ A N D S O U L C

TRIVIA QUESTION:

The heart is an important organ in our bodies. It's also something else. What is it?
Put the uncircled letters in order on the blanks.

ANSWER:

___ ___ ___ ___   ___ ___ ___ ___ ___

___ ___ ___   ___ ___ ___ ___ ___   ___ ___ ___ ___.

RIDDLE SUDOKU

These sudoku puzzles use letters instead of numbers. Fill in the squares so that the six letters appear only once in each row, column, and 2x3 box. Then read the yellow squares to find out the answer to the riddle.

LETTERS: I L P S T U

	L		S	I	
I			T		
			P		
	T				
	U				I
	P	I		T	

RIDDLE

- We are flowers that grow from bulbs.

- Our name comes from a word that means "turban."

- Many of us are grown in Holland.

- We usually have one flower per stem.

What are we?

RIDDLE

- I'm in the gourd family.

- Among my many types are pumpkin and zucchini.

- I'm also a verb that means "to crush or smash."

What am I?

LETTERS: A H Q S U Y

				Q	
U		Y			
	H				Q
Q				H	
			Y		A
	S				

106

Art Monsterpieces

The Fleezles™ are a typical family of monsters who love to star in logic puzzles!

Grand Fleezles   Sister   Brother   Dad   Mom

Today is the Monster Art Show! Each Fleezle created a work of art for this friendly contest. Using the clues below, figure out which Fleezle made which artwork and won which ribbon. Put an O in each box that must be true in the chart and an X in each box that can't be true.
TIP: Fill in all three sections of the chart as you read the clues. It will help you solve the puzzle.

CLUES

1. Mom's monsterpiece was closer to first place than *Whistling Mummy*, but it didn't do as well as *Spooky Night*.

2. The painters of *Spooky Night* and *The Screamer* have facial hair.

3. The sculptor of *Headless Thinker* finished in third place and does NOT have four hands.

4. A three-legged Fleezle painted *Whistling Mummy*, which finished one place better than *The Screamer*.

5. The Fleezle who wears a hat is scared of ghosts, so he didn't paint *Spooky Night*.

SPOOKY NIGHT

	Headless Thinker	Moaner Lisa	The Screamer	Spooky Night	Whistling Mummy	1st place	2nd place	3rd place	4th place	5th place
Mom										
Dad										
Sister										
Brother										
Grand Fleezles										
1st place										
2nd place										
3rd place										
4th place										
5th place										

THE SCREAMER

HEADLESS THINKER

MOANER LISA

WHISTLING MUMMY

WRITTEN BY ANDREW BRISMAN;
ART BY JACOB CHABOT

School Spirit

Each of these scenes contains **12 hidden objects**, which are listed at the right. Find each object in one of the scenes, then cross it off the list.

Each object is hidden only once. Can you find them all?

arrow
candle
coffeepot
elephant
fish

funnel
ice-cream bar
ladder
light bulb
magnet

needle
oilcan
owl
pennant
ring

roller skate
ruler
slice of
  watermelon
sock

spatula
spoon
suitcase
top hat
umbrella
yo-yo

START

Peak Performance

Help this skier find the way from the top of the mountain at START to the lodge at FINISH.

SKI RENTAL

LODGE

FINISH

ART AND MAZE BY ROBERT PRINCE

111

Beware This Crisscross

Bwahahahaha! The 30 words or phrases below are different ways of saying *scary*. They fit in the grid in only one way. Use the number of letters in each word or phrase as a clue to where it might fit. We started you off with *HAUNTED*.

5 LETTERS

EERIE

HAIRY

WEIRD

6 LETTERS

CREEPY

GRISLY

7 LETTERS

FEARFUL

GHASTLY

GHOSTLY

HAUNTED

MACABRE

OMINOUS

STRANGE

8 LETTERS

ALARMING

CHILLING

DREADFUL

GHOULISH

GRUESOME

SHOCKING

9 LETTERS

GROTESQUE

HARROWING

WORRISOME

10 LETTERS

DIABOLICAL

FORBIDDING

TERRIFYING

UNSETTLING

11 LETTERS

FRIGHTENING

HAIR-RAISING

12 LETTERS

NERVE-RACKING

13 LETTERS

BLOODCURDLING

HEART-STOPPING

HAUNTED

113

Freeze Frame

Glide around this rink and find the **25 differences** between these two pages.

ART BY RICH POWELL

Hidden Pictures

6 by Six

Each of these small scenes contains **6 hidden objects** from the list below. Some objects are hidden in more than one scene. Can you find the 6 hidden objects in each scene?

HIDDEN OBJECT LIST

boomerang **(3)**	olive **(4)**
carrot **(3)**	paintbrush **(4)**
crescent moon **(4)**	peanut **(2)**
feather **(2)**	ruler **(4)**
golf club **(4)**	slice of pie **(2)**
mushroom **(2)**	waffle **(2)**

The numbers tell you how many times each object is hidden.

THE SPEEDSTER

ART BY NEIL NUMBERMAN

HINKS PINKS

Read each clue below. The answers are Hinks Pinks, pairs of words that rhyme. We did one to get you started.

HINK PINK:
Each answer is a pair of one-syllable rhyming words.

1. Rodent husband:
   <u>MOUSE</u> <u>SPOUSE</u>

2. Geography song:
   _____ _____

HINKY PINKY:
Each answer is a pair of two-syllable rhyming words.

3. Smelly finger: _____ _____

4. Tortoise obstacle: _____ _____

HINKETY PINKETY:
The answer is a pair of three-syllable rhyming words.

5. Voting choice:
   _____ _____

BONUS ROUND:

1. **Hink Pink:** Slippery fowl: _____ _____

2. **Hinky Pinky:** Horrible duo:
   _____ _____

3. **Hinkety Pinkety:** Sea cow conceitedness:
   _____ _____

Going in Circles

Use the clues below to fill in the boxes of this spiral—**but there's a twist**: the last letter of each word is also the first letter of the next word. Use the linking letters to help you spin all the way to the center. We did the first one for you.

1. Bed for a baby
4. Cover on your bed that keeps you warm
10. You take a bath in it
12. Place in the house where you sleep
18. Large, round, white object in the night sky
21. Person who likes to stay up late; also a nocturnal bird
28. Bedtime song for a baby
34. To open your mouth wide when you're tired
37. Bad dream
45. You close these to sleep.
48. Animals some people count to fall asleep
52. You lay your head on it.
57. What you do when you're done sleeping
62. Clothes you wear to bed
68. Soft shoes you might wear around the house
75. They twinkle in the night sky.
79. Sack you sleep in while you're camping
89. What you say before going to bed: "_____ night"
92. What your mind is doing while you're sleeping

C R I B

Bark and Park

This driving school gets a five-paw rating. And you will, too, by solving the puzzle. First use the secret code to figure out what objects are hidden in the scene. Then use that list to find the **16 hidden objects** in the big picture.

1 R E E A → B O O K

2 S E C R → ☐☐☐☐

3 A Y J U → ☐☐☐☐

4 H K B U H → ☐☐☐☐☐

5 S Q H H E J → ☐☐☐☐☐☐

6 D U U T B U → ☐☐☐☐☐☐

7 J U Q S K F → ☐☐☐☐☐☐

8 U D L U B E F U → ☐☐☐☐☐☐☐☐

9 W E B V   S B K R → ☐☐☐☐   ☐☐☐☐

10 C U W Q F X E D U → ☐☐☐☐☐☐☐☐☐

11 J E E J X R H K I X → ☐☐☐☐☐☐☐☐☐☐

12 R K J J U H   A D Y V U → ☐☐☐☐☐☐   ☐☐☐☐☐

13 X E S A U O   I J Y S A → ☐☐☐☐☐☐   ☐☐☐☐☐

14 S H U I S U D J   C E E D → ☐☐☐☐☐☐☐☐   ☐☐☐☐

I B Y S U   E V → ☐☐☐☐☐   ☐☐

15 F Y P P Q → ☐☐☐☐☐

F Y U S U   E V → ☐☐☐☐☐   ☐☐

16 F E F S E H D → ☐☐☐☐☐☐☐

CODE CRACKER

A=K	H=R	O=Y	V=F
B=L	I=S	P=Z	W=G
C=M	J=T	Q=A	X=H
D=N	K=U	R=B	Y=I
E=O	L=V	S=C	Z=J
F=P	M=W	T=D	
G=Q	N=X	U=E	

Party of Three

The numbered scenes can each be described by three words that start with the same letter. For example, the first scene is *FARMER FIXING FOUNTAIN*. The other scenes use different letters (not in number order): *CCC*, *DDD*, *EEE*, *GGG*, *HHH*, *KKK*, *LLL*, and *MMM*. Can you figure them out? Write your answers on a piece of paper.

ART BY SOPHIE GOLDSTEIN

FLOCK
TOGETHER

There is more than meets the eye in this photo. Focus in, and see if you can find all **18 objects** hiding here.

boot	needle
bowling pin	pencil
dog	rat
dolphin	shoe
fish	shovel
glove	slice of cake
heart	sunglasses
ice-cream cone	teacup
mitten	toothbrush

Ready, Set, SLOW!

The Annual Tortoise Marathon will take a looooong time to complete, especially because the tortoises don't know the correct route. Figure out the one sequence of paths from START to FINISH that totals exactly 26 miles without running on the same path twice. No rush!

Spaced Out

Don't be alarmed, but there's a new kid at the science fair this year. There are also **24 hidden objects**. Can you find them all?

- artist's brush
- balloon
- baseball
- book
- canoe
- dog bone
- drinking straw
- eraser
- eyeglasses
- high-heeled shoe
- hockey stick
- ladder
- lamp
- lighthouse
- pennant
- pitchfork
- pointy hat
- ruler
- sailboat
- saltshaker
- shovel
- sugar bowl
- toothbrush
- wristwatch

BONUS EXHIBIT: Can you find 5 batteries in this scene?

ART BY RON ZALME

Hidden in Plain Sight

Can you find the **12 rubber ducks** hidden in this photo?

SIZE UP In Orbit

These planets look the same size here, but they're actually very different. Can you rank them in size order? Put a 1 next to the smallest and a 6 next to the largest.

Mars

Venus

Mercury

Jupiter

Earth

Neptune

NUMBER CRUNCH

People, you know how to add, subtract, multiply, and divide, right? Then you can play calcudoku! Now give me 20 squats. I said *NOW!*

HOW TO PLAY:

- To complete a game, each number will appear only once in a row and only once in a column, like in sudoku.

- The set of squares inside the heavy lines is called a cage. Each cage shows a bold number and a math sign. The math sign (+, -, x, /) tells you to add, subtract, multiply, or divide.

- The cage's bold number is the answer to the equation. For example, "12x" means that the numbers in the cage's squares must equal 12 when they are multiplied.

HERE'S AN EXAMPLE:

The only possible numbers for 2/ in this puzzle are 2 and 1. You may not know which number goes where, so write the numbers down as possibilities in the corners of the squares.

It's good to start with the multiplication cages. **18x** can only be 3x3x2. And just like in sudoku, you can't put the 3s in the same row or column (but they can be in the same cage).

2/ 1	2	4+ 3
18x 2	3	1
3	1- 1	2

Since the 2/ cage uses the numbers 2 and 1, the top square of the 4+ cage must be a 3.

An equal sign after a number means that you should put that number in the square.

The order of the numbers in a cage doesn't matter, but there's only one order that works in the finished puzzle.

CUTE 3x3 PUZZLE
(NUMBERS 1–3)

2x		9x
1-		
	3+	

FRIENDLY 4x4 PUZZLE
(NUMBERS 1–4)

2x		6x	1-
	4=		
1-	5+	1=	7+

FIERCE 5x5 PUZZLE
(NUMBERS 1–5)

10x		5+		7+
3-	5=	9x	20x	
10+		3-	3/	
			9+	

WRITTEN BY ANDREW BRISMAN; ACE ILLUSTRATED BY R. SIKORYAK;
PHOTO BY EMRAH TURUDU/EXACTOSTOCK/SUPERSTOCK (CHALKBOARD)

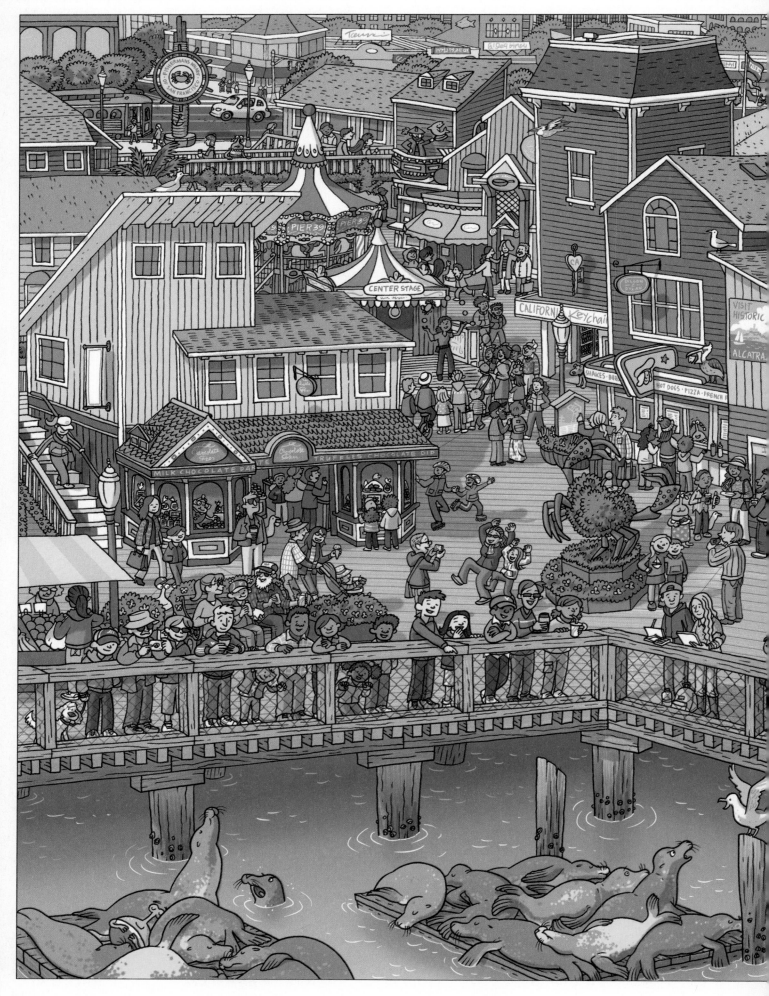

Class Trek: Quarkle Middle School Visits Earth

D-Leader and the students in her out-of-this-world cultures class are on another field trip. They've left Planet Q to visit Fisherman's Wharf in San Francisco. As usual, all the students got lost in a flash. Can you help D-Leader find her **6 students** in the big scene? Then look for the items on their field-trip checklist. Check off each one you find.

Can you find my students in the crowd?

J-KUB B-BOP KAY-T C-YAH N-DROO BUG-Z

FIELD-TRIP CHECKLIST

- [ ] 5 seagulls
- [ ] 4 crabs
- [ ] 2 sailboats
- [ ] 4 cups of coffee
- [ ] 2 blue tote bags
- [ ] 2 babies
- [ ] 1 yellow backpack
- [ ] 2 inline skaters
- [ ] 2 purple jackets
- [ ] 3 ice-cream cones
- [ ] 2 balloons
- [ ] 1 unicycle
- [ ] 8 ponytails
- [ ] 3 fish
- [ ] 2 pelicans
- [ ] 2 hot dogs

ART BY CHUCK DILLON

Match-Up↑ Queens

Can you find the **4 pairs** of identical cards, the **3 cards** that are exactly alike, and the **1 card** that has no match? HINT: The bottom half of each card is a mirror image of the top.

1

2

3

7

8

9

Fill in your answers here.

Pair: ___ and ___

Pair: ___ and ___

Pair: ___ and ___

Pair: ___ and ___

Trio: ___, ___, and ___

Single: ___

Sweet Summer

Quick! Study this page for one minute. Then turn to page 140 to test your memory!

Picture THIS

The words in each box show a common phrase. Pay attention to how the words are arranged to figure out the phrase. For example, in the first one, the word *DROP* is inside the words *THE BUCKET*. So the answer is *DROP IN THE BUCKET*. Can you get them all?

1

THEdropBUCKET

ANSWER: DROP IN THE BUCKET

2

BROKE

ANSWER:

3

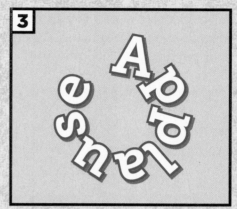

ANSWER:

4

SUDDEN P
O
U
R

ANSWER:

5

DUMPS DUMPS DUMPS
DUMPS DUMPS DUMPS
DUMPS DUMPS DUMPS
DUMPS **DOWN** DUMPS
DUMPS DUMPS DUMPS
DUMPS DUMPS DUMPS

ANSWER:

6

X SPOT

ANSWER:

BRAIN SQUEEZE

Use these tricky questions to stump your family and friends.

1 If it takes six men six days to dig six holes, how long will it take three men to dig half a hole?

2 What object do you throw out when you want to use it, but take in when you don't want to use it?

TEST YOUR MEMORY

Did you study the scene on page 138? Now see if you can answer these questions. Circle your responses. No peeking!

• • • • • • • • • • • • • • • • • • •

1. How many penguins are in the picture?

    4   5   6

• • • • • • • • • • • • • • • • • • •

2. How are some penguins holding their ice-cream cones?

ON STICKS   ON ICICLES

ON LIGHTNING BOLTS

• • • • • • • • • • • • • • • • • • •

3. Which is the correct color of the cooler?

• • • • • • • • • • • • • • • • • • •

4. Which two items are NOT in the picture?

LANTERN   PLAID BLANKET
MILKSHAKE   TENT

• • • • • • • • • • • • • • • • • • •

5. There's a puzzle piece hidden on page 138. Where is it?

ON AN ICE-CREAM CONE

ON A PENGUIN'S STOMACH

ON THE ICE

Splish, Splash, SEARCH

Take the plunge into this watery word search. Circle the 31 words about water hidden in this grid. Look up, down, across, backward, and diagonally. The uncircled letters answer the trivia question.

WORD LIST

ATLANTIC	FISH	RIVER
BAY	FOUNTAIN	SEA
BROOK	GUPPY	SHARK
CLAMS	INLET	SNORKEL
CORAL	LAKE	SURFING
CREEK	LAPS	TANK
DEW	OCEAN	WATER
DIVER	PACIFIC	WAVES
DOWNPOUR	POOL	WHALE
DRIZZLE	PUDDLE	
FINS	RAIN	

TRIVIA QUESTION:

What word looks the same right side up and upside down? Put the uncircled letters in order on the blanks.

ANSWER: ___ ___ ___   ___ ___ ___ ___

___ ___ ___ ___ ___   ___ ___ ___

___ ___ ___   ___ ___ ___ ___

___ ___ ___ ___ ___ ___ ___

___ ___ ___ .

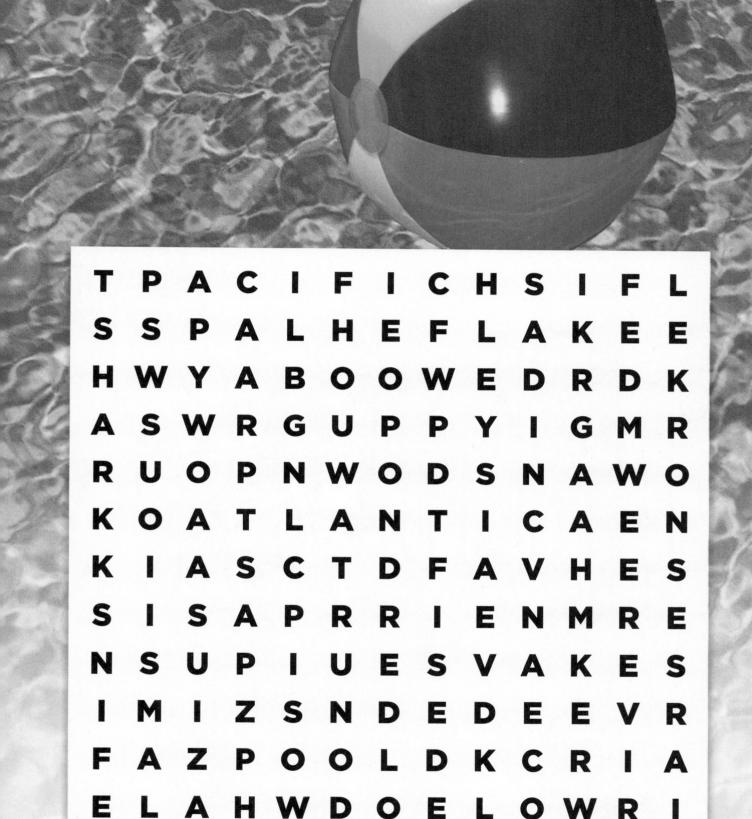

```
T P A C I F I C H S I F L
S S P A L H E F L A K E E
H W Y A B O O W E D R D K
A S W R G U P P Y I G M R
R U O P N W O D S N A W O
K O A T L A N T I C A E N
K I A S C T D F A V H E S
S I S A P R R I E N M R E
N S U P I U E S V A K E S
I M I Z S N D E D E E V R
F A Z P O O L D K C R I A
E L A H W D O E L O W R I
E C O R A L W A T E R N N
```

Better LATE Than Never

Some animals in town are running late. But that's not all. Thirteen items or actions in this scene rhyme with the word *LATE*. For example, the first one is *DATE*. Can you figure out the rest? We numbered them to help you out.

ART BY JEF CZEKAJ

PIZZA   PASTA

TAXI

$1/mile

THIS SIDE UP

Marching Madness

Oh, say, can you see the 25 differences between these two pictures?

Can you find these details in the picture below?

The Legion OF Super Solvers™

This super trio (from left, the Gentleman Gorilla™, Count Yoga™, and the Human Turnip™) uses puzzle powers to keep the world safe from wrong answers.

THE CASE OF THE HOPEFUL HERO

A young superhero wants to join the Super Solvers. But first, he needs to impress them with his puzzling abilities. So he created three puzzles that will reveal his name. Can you solve the puzzles and learn the identity of the hopeful hero?

Super Scramble

The mystery hero has taken the names of the Super Solvers and scrambled each one into three words. For each Super Solver, find the three words in the list below whose letters make his or her complete name (ignore word spaces). The leftover word is your key word.

Note: Each word is used only once. Some words may seem to work with more than one Super Solver, but there is only one unique, three-word solution for each hero's name.

CON	GUY	LINGO	NUT	RAIN
GEAR	HUMP	MANAGER	OAT	TELL

Count Yoga

1. _____ 2. _____ 3. _____

Gentleman Gorilla

1. _____ 2. _____ 3. _____

> I APPRECIATE THIS FELLOW'S CHOICE OF HEROES—EVEN IF THE ANAGRAMS ARE SCRAMBLING MY BRAIN A BIT.

Human Turnip

1. _____ 2. _____ 3. _____

Write the leftover word.

KEY WORD: _____ _____ _____

The Gentleman Gorilla

The Big Sipper

The mystery hero has a gift for Count Yoga at the end of this maze. Find the only path through the maze from START to FINISH. Then write down the letters you passed through in order. That's your key word.

Count Yoga

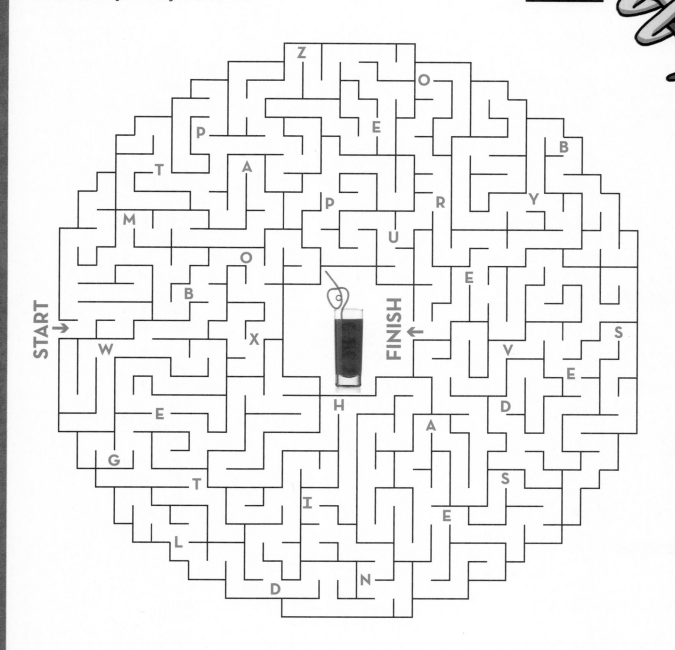

Write the letters you passed through in order.

KEY WORD: _____ _____ _____ _____ _____ _____

WRITTEN BY ANDREW AND LEV BRISMAN; ART BY R. SIKORYAK; PHOTO BY SRDJAN STEFANOVIC/ISTOCK

Oh, Say, Can You See?

Each country on the left has had some letters removed from its name. Those missing letters, when read in order, spell the name of one of the objects on the right. Can you make all the correct matches to fill in the country names? You'll have one leftover object. That's your key word.

The Human Turnip

WHAT, NO TURNIPISTAN?! OH, WELL. I STILL THINK THIS NEW HERO MAKES A NICE PUZZLE.

1 u_N_It_E_d _S_T_ATES

2 __OUT__ K__R__A

3 TUR__ __ __

4 NET__ ERL __ __ __S

5 UNITED __ __ __ __DOM

6 __R__ __CE

7 __OL __ __ __IA

8 __ __ __ADA

A

B

C

D

E

F

G

H

I

Write the name of the only object that's left.

KEY WORD: _____ _____ _____ _____

The Mystery Hero Revealed!

Place the key words in the blanks. Then copy each letter to the same numbered square below to identify the hero.

THE GENTLEMAN GORILLA'S KEY WORD:

___ ___ ___ ___
6   3   11 8

COUNT YOGA'S KEY WORD:

___ ___ ___ ___ ___ ___
9   4   2   5   12 10

THE HUMAN TURNIP'S KEY WORD:

___ ___ ___ ___
1   14 7   13

THE HERO IS:

| 1 | 2 | 3 | | 4 | 5 | 6 | 7 | 8 | | 9 | 10 | 11 | 12 | 13 | 14 |

Now that you know the enthusiastic hero's name, draw what he looks like here.

NEW HERO!

Hidden Pieces

MENTAL BLOCKS

Can you find these **11 jigsaw pieces** in this photo of plastic bricks?

Hot and Cold

Each of these scenes contains **12 hidden objects**, which are listed at the right. Find each object in one of the scenes, then cross it off the list.

DADDY-O
THE
PATIO

acorn

adhesive bandage

artist's brush

banana

baseball cap

broccoli

carrot

crescent moon

envelope

eyeglasses

fishing net

harmonica

heart

hockey stick

ice-cream bar

lollipop

needle

olive

popcorn

ruler

spoon

tack

top hat

wishbone

Such a Nice Crisscross

The list below is made up of 30 words that can all mean *NICE*. They fit in the grid in only one way. Use the number of letters in each word as a clue to where it might fit. We did one to get you started.

6 LETTERS
CARING
GENIAL
GENTLE
~~HUMANE~~
TENDER

7 LETTERS
AMIABLE
CORDIAL
HELPFUL

8 LETTERS
FRIENDLY
GENEROUS
MERCIFUL
OBLIGING
OUTGOING
PLEASANT
SOCIABLE
VIRTUOUS

9 LETTERS
CONGENIAL
COURTEOUS
SENSITIVE

10 LETTERS
ALTRUISTIC
BENEVOLENT
CHARITABLE
CHIVALROUS
HOSPITABLE
MUNIFICENT
NEIGHBORLY
THOUGHTFUL

11 LETTERS
GOOD-NATURED
SYMPATHETIC

13 LETTERS
UNDERSTANDING

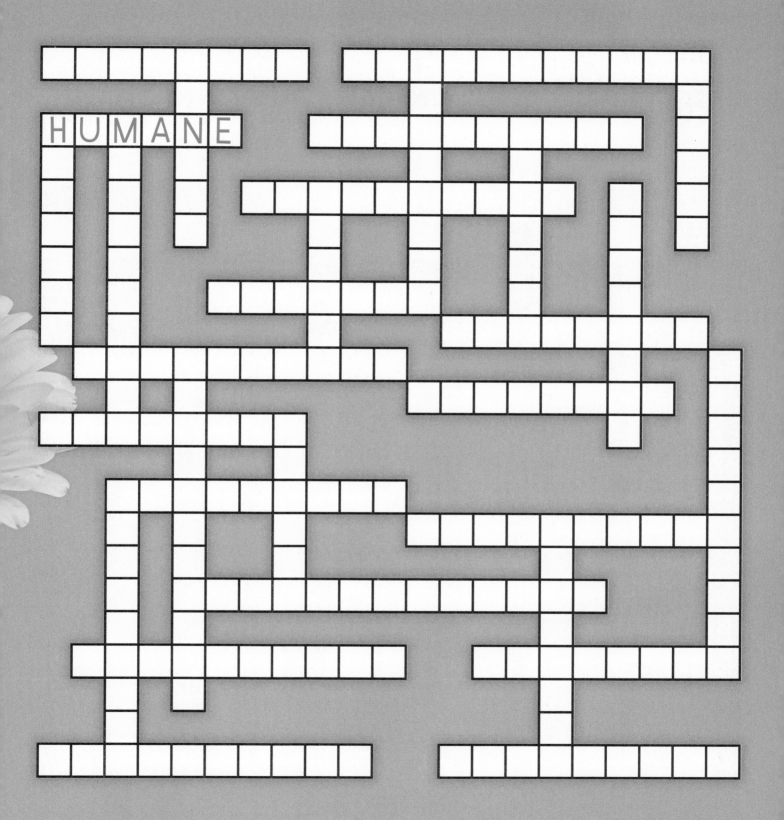

HUMANE

A Hop, a Skip, and a Jump

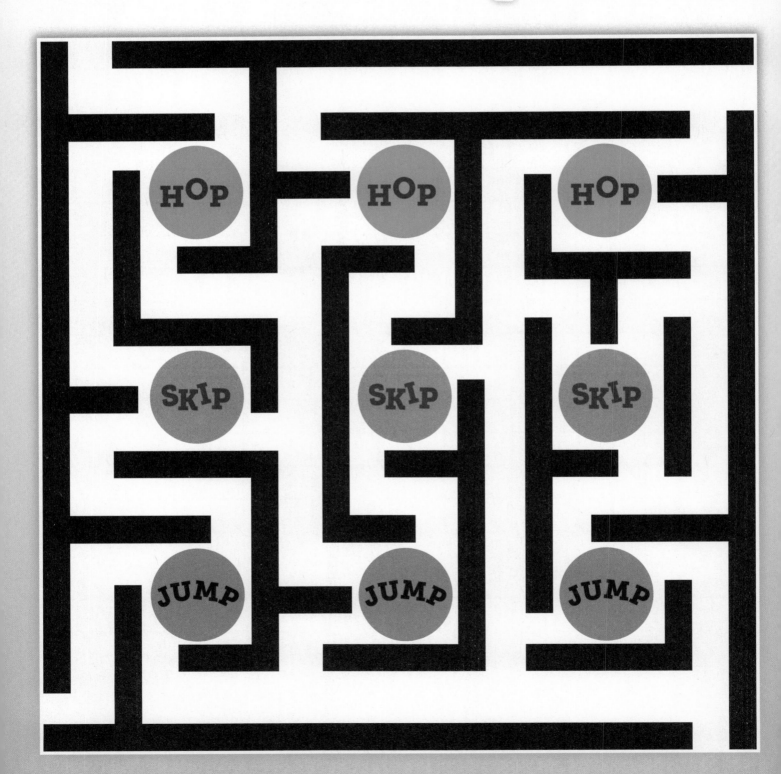

Getting to the end of the mazes below requires you to hop, skip, and jump three times in each one. Start the maze on page 156 from any of the entrances—but some won't work. Pass through all the hops, skips, and jumps in this order: first hop, then skip, then jump. Continue that order two more times. You may not retrace your path.

When you get out of the first maze, go to the next one, below. Travel through it in the same way. Good luck!

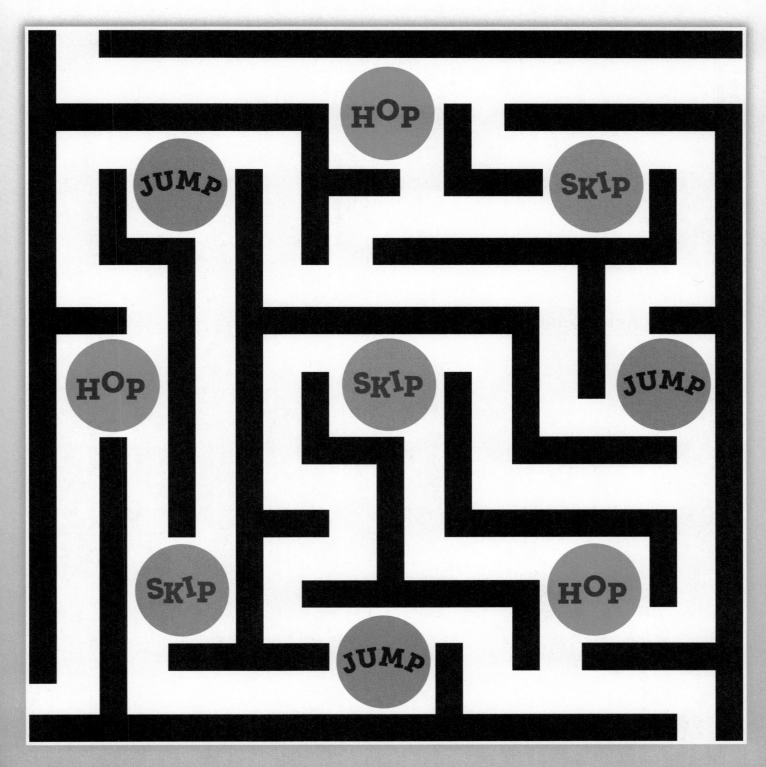

SIZE UP Fetch!

These dogs look about the same size here, but they're actually very different. Which of these breeds is, on average, the biggest? Put them in size order, with 1 for the smallest breed and 6 for the biggest.

DACHSHUND

LABRADOR RETRIEVER

YORKSHIRE TERRIER

BORDER COLLIE

CHIHUAHUA

BERNESE MOUNTAIN DOG

Body Language

The missing letters in each word spell out the name of a body part. Cross the words off the list as you fill in each answer. We gave you a hand with the first one.

WORD LIST

ARM	EAR	HAIR	INTESTINES	NECK	STOMACH
ARTERY	ELBOW	HEAD	LEG	SKIN	TOE
BRAIN	~~EYE~~	HIP	LUNG	SPINE	

1. Old Faithful is one. G <u>E</u> <u>Y</u> S <u>E</u> R

2. Branch of the military __ __ __ Y

3. A nick or crack, as in a teacup C __ __ __

4. Gloomy D R __ __ __ Y

5. Wagon W H E __ __ __ A R R __ __

6. Carry __ __ T __

7. It unclogs the toilet. P __ __ __ __ E R

8. Stylish E __ __ __ A N T

9. Warmed __ __ __ T E __

10. Defensive football player L I __ __ B A __ __ __ E R

11. Four times a year Q U __ __ __ __ __ __ L __

12. Out of control __ __ Y W __ __ E

13. Requesting A __ __ __ __ G

14. Stopping the car __ __ __ K __ __ G

15. Crunchiness C R I __ __ __ __ __ S S

16. Fascinating concepts __ __ __ __ E R __ __ __ __ __ __ __ G I D __ A __

17. "Halt the parade!" "__ __ __ P __ __ R __ __ I N G!"

Hidden Pictures® SUPER CHALLENGE

Game Night

Anna invited all her friends over for a game night. You can play along and search for the **24 hidden objects** in this scene.

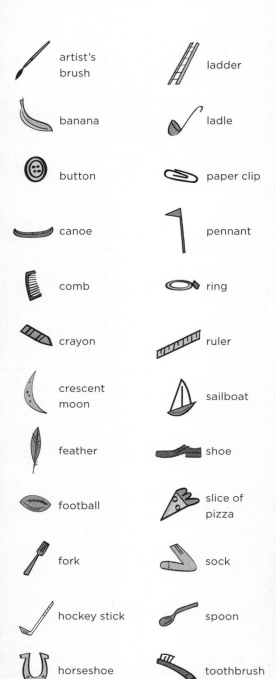

- artist's brush
- banana
- button
- canoe
- comb
- crayon
- crescent moon
- feather
- football
- fork
- hockey stick
- horseshoe
- ladder
- ladle
- paper clip
- pennant
- ring
- ruler
- sailboat
- shoe
- slice of pizza
- sock
- spoon
- toothbrush

BONUS GAME: Can you find 5 pairs of dice in this scene?

The BIG and

ACROSS

1 SMALL ___ (chitchat)

5 Opposite of night

8 "Do it ___ !" (once more)

10 "I don't like your ___ of voice, young man."

11 "I'm ___ doing this. I've never done it before." (2 words)

12 People who often write in rhyme

13 World ___ I and II

15 Abbreviation for the month after Sept.

18 Threw, in football

22 Don't tell the truth

23 Secret agent

24 One plus one

25 Frontiersman Boone

27 "Not ___ ." (up until now)

28 Stinging insects

30 Frequently

33 Dog or wolf cries

38 BIG ___ (Sasquatch)

39 Enthusiastic cry, like "Yippee!" or "Yee-haw!"

40 SMALL ___ (little kid)

41 SMALL ___ (opposite of big city)

DOWN

1 Khaki-colored

2 What the number of birthday candles represents

3 ___ enforcement (police)

4 First-aid ___

5 Female deer

6 Unwanted bug at a picnic

7 Opposite of *no*

9 This very moment

10 Throw, as a horseshoe or beanbag

12 What people might do in church

14 The BIG ___ (nickname for New York City)

15 Opposite of young

16 Abbreviation for Central Intelligence Agency

17 The BIG ___ (college football conference)

19 Pig's home

20 Female sheep

21 It comes before "com" or "edu" in an e-mail address

23 "Have you ___ the new movie yet?"

26 "___ you five cents I can do this puzzle." (2 words)

29 Bashful; timid

30 Opposite of *on*

31 "___ He's a Jolly Good Fellow"

32 Typical birthday present

34 Grain in a granola bar

35 "___ , what, when, where, and why?"

36 Opposite of high

37 Father's baby boy

SMALL Crossword

There are six BIG and small clues in this puzzle. HINT: If you don't know the answer to a clue, look at the other clues that are around it, both across and down, or try another part of the puzzle and come back to the tough clue later.

11. N E W T O

Hidden Pictures

6 by Six

Each of these small scenes contains 6 hidden objects from the list below. Some objects are hidden in more than one scene. Can you find the 6 hidden objects in each scene?

HIDDEN OBJECT LIST

envelope (4)	radish (2)
fishhook (2)	rolling pin (3)
fork (3)	ruler (3)
needle (3)	slice of pizza (3)
paper clip (3)	tack (3)
piece of popcorn (4)	toothbrush (3)

The numbers tell you how many times each object is hidden.

BONUS MATCH
Two scenes contain the exact same set of hidden objects. Can you find that matching pair?

ART BY NEIL NUMBERMAN

Match-Up ↑ Cupcakes

Can you find the **4 pairs** of identical cupcakes, the **3 cupcakes** that are exactly alike, and the **1 cupcake** that has no match?

Fill in your answers here.

Pair: ___ and ___

Pair: ___ and ___

Pair: ___ and ___

Pair: ___ and ___

Trio: ___, ___, and ___

Single: ___

4

5

6

10

11

12

ARTIST AT WORK

There is more than meets the eye in this photo. Focus in, and see if you can find all **14 objects** hiding here.

 banana

mushroom

candle

needle

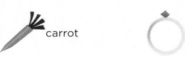 carrot

ring

 eyeglasses

sailboat

 fish

shoe

 ice-cream cone

spatula

 ladybug

toothbrush

RIDDLE

These sudoku puzzles use letters instead of numbers. Fill in the squares so that the six letters appear only once in each row, column, and 2x3 box. Then read the yellow squares to find out the answer to the riddle.

LETTERS: A C D F N R

			F	A	D
	F	N	D		C
		C			N
	C		R		
	R	F		N	

RIDDLE

- I am the second-largest country in the world in total area. (Russia is first.)
- I have the world's longest coastline.
- I have two official languages: English and French.

What country am I?

RIDDLE

What can you never eat for breakfast?

LETTERS: C D E I N R

					E
E			R	D	
	C			R	
	D	E			I
	R				C
		I			

WRITTEN BY ANDREW BRISMAN

Fleezle Fitness

The Fleezles™ are a typical family of monsters who love to star in logic puzzles!

Grand Fleezles   Sister   Brother   Dad   Mom

The Fleezles like to work up a sweat in different fitness classes at their local gym. Using the clues below, figure out each Fleezle's class and its starting time. Put an O in each box in the chart that must be true and an X in each box that can't be true.

TIP: Fill in all three sections of the chart as you read the clues. It will help you solve the puzzle.

CLUES

1. The Grand Fleezles can't do Trampoline Aerobics (their heads might knock together), and their class starts an hour after Super Cycling.

2. Brother likes to be the first Fleezle to get sweaty at the gym.

3. A one-eyed Fleezle is focused on building muscles in Strength and Tone.

4. Dad is too sleepy to start a class before 10:30 a.m.

5. Sister's class is immediately after Mom's class and immediately before Ballet for Beginners.

	Ballet for Beginners	Power Yoga	Strength and Tone	Super Cycling	Trampoline Aerobics	10:00 a.m.	10:15 a.m.	10:30 a.m.	10:45 a.m.	11:00 a.m.
Mom										
Dad										
Sister										
Brother										
Grand Fleezles										
10:00 a.m.					
10:15 a.m.					
10:30 a.m.					
10:45 a.m.					
11:00 a.m.					

WRITTEN BY ANDREW BRISMAN; ART BY JACOB CHABOT

Cat City

Quick! Study this page for one minute. Then turn to page 174 to test your memory!

Picture THIS

The words in each box show a common phrase. Pay attention to how the words are arranged to figure out the phrase. For example, in the first one, the word *SLEEP* is on top of *IT*. So the answer is *SLEEP ON IT*. Can you get them all?

1

ANSWER: SLEEP ON IT

2

WEAR
LONG

ANSWER:

3

ANSWER:

4

GO
BOARD

ANSWER:

5

TAKE TAKE

ANSWER:

6

ANSWER:

BRAIN SQUEEZE

Use these tricky questions to stump your family and friends.

1 You're in a room with three light switches, all set to OFF. Each switch controls one of three light bulbs in the basement, but you don't know which one. How can you figure out which light switch controls which light? You can turn on any switches, but you're only allowed to go to the basement once.

2 What word becomes shorter when you add two letters to it?

TEST YOUR MEMORY

Did you study the scene on page 172? Now see if you can answer these questions. Circle your responses. No peeking!

• • • • • • • • • • • • • • • • • • •

1. How many cats are in the taxi?

   2   3   1

• • • • • • • • • • • • • • • • • • •

2. What is the waiter serving at the restaurant?

   CHICKEN   FISH   ICE CREAM

• • • • • • • • • • • • • • • • • • •

3. What is the correct color of the bus driver's cap?

• • • • • • • • • • • • • • • • • • •

4. How many dogs can we see riding the bus (not counting the driver)?

   7   8   9

• • • • • • • • • • • • • • • • • • •

5. There's a puzzle piece hidden on page 172. Where is it?

   ON THE BUS
   ON A CAT
   ON THE STREET

Paws and Claws

Twenty-six animals—from A to Z—got lost in this grid. Look up, down, across, backward, and diagonally, and circle each animal you find. The uncircled letters answer the trivia question.

WORD LIST

ANTELOPE	JAGUAR	SKUNK
BADGER	KOALA	TOUCAN
CAMEL	LLAMA	UMBRELLABIRD
DONKEY	MARTEN	VULTURE
EAGLE	NEWT	WOLF
FOX	OCELOT	XENOPS
GOAT	PORCUPINE	YAK
HERON	QUAIL	ZEBRA
IGUANA	REINDEER	

```
J B O C E L O T T S H E Q
U A I C K B R O P C V U Z
W D G N F O A O X A U M E
H G J U U M N M P M L B B
S E O V A E A G L E T R R
F R R L X R E R F L U E A
T O L O R T H L T E R L N
L O X A N G O A T E E L T
S K U N K W I G U A N A E
P O R C U P I N E N Z B L
K O A L A D O N K E Y I O
Q U A I L N Y D O W A R P
R E I N D E E R G T K D E
```

TRIVIA QUESTION:

What's a sentence that uses all 26 letters of the alphabet?

Put the uncircled letters in order on the blanks.

ANSWER: _____ _____ _____   _____ _____ _____ _____

_____ _____ _____ _____ _____   _____ _____ _____   _____ _____ _____ _____

_____ _____ _____   _____ _____ _____   _____ _____ _____

_____ _____ _____ .

Hidden in Plain Sight

Can you find the **12 toy dinosaurs** hidden in this photo?

Stee-rike!

Before you get rolling, see if you can find the **27 hidden object**s in this scene.

FIND THESE OBJECTS: acorn, baseball cap, boomerang, bowl, cracker, drum, envelope, funnel, gumdrop, heart, horseshoe, jar, lemon, needle, peanut, pea pod, piece of popcorn, purse, ring, ruler, shuttlecock, slice of pizza, star, stick of gum, teacup, tweezers, and worm.

ART BY DIANA ZOURELIAS

Pizza or Ice Cream?

Which one is better? It's a tough decision, but these mazes will help. Start the maze on this page in one of the three possible entrances (but there are only two that will work), pass through all the pizza and ice cream pictures, and then exit the maze in one of the three possible exits. You must alternate between pizza and ice cream as you go, and you may not retrace or cross your path.

When you get out of the maze on the left, choose one of the entrances below to start the new maze (again, only two entrances work). Go through the maze in the same way, alternating between pizza and ice cream. The last item you go through before exiting is your decision—at least for today!

Clown Food

Welcome to the Giggle Diner! Here you can order amusing food and solve this puzzle. First use the clues below to figure out the words. Each word is a hidden object to look for in the big scene. Once you've found the **13 hidden objects**, then transfer the letters with numbers into the correct spaces to learn the punch line to the joke.

1 It opens a lock.

<u>K E Y</u>
    1

2 Check one out of the library.

__ __ __ __ __
    2

3 You might wave one on the Fourth of July.

__ __ __ __
    3

4 **A** tasty nut for squirrels

__ __ __ __ __
    4

5 A measuring stick

__ __ __ __ __
    5

6 A boa constrictor or copperhead

__ __ __ __ __
    6

7 Use this to eat soup.

__ __ __ __ __
    7

8 Rabbits love to crunch this vegetable.

__ __ __ __ __ __
    8

9 Like a glove, but without fingers

__ __ __ __ __ __
    9

10 Thread goes through its eye.

__ __ __ __ __ __
    10

11 "Birds of a _____ flock together."

__ __ __ __ __ __ __
    11

12 Mail a letter in this.

__ __ __ __ __ __ __ __
    12

13 Your dentist may give you one to use at home.

__ __ __ __ __ __ __ __ __ __
    13

What do clowns like to eat for breakfast?

__ __ __ __ __ __ __ __ __ __
12 3 3 13 8 2 2 6 12 10

y_
__ __ __ __ __ __ __ __ __ __ __
11 5 4 4 1 13 9 10 12 5 7

ART BY MIKE MORAN

Ride and Seek

Which ride do you want to try first? Before you get in line, find at least **25 differences** between these two pictures.

Name This Crisscross

Do you see your last name in the list below? If you do, you have one of the 40 most common last names in the United States.* The names fit in the grid in only one way. Use the number of letters in each name as a clue to where it might fit. We started you off with three.

3 LETTERS
LEE

4 LETTERS
HILL
KING

5 LETTERS
ALLEN
~~BROWN~~
CLARK
DAVIS
JONES
LEWIS
LOPEZ
MOORE
PEREZ
SCOTT
SMITH
WHITE
YOUNG

6 LETTERS
FLORES
GARCIA
HARRIS
MARTIN
~~MILLER~~
NGUYEN
TAYLOR
THOMAS
TORRES
~~WALKER~~
WILSON
WRIGHT

7 LETTERS
JACKSON
JOHNSON
RAMIREZ
SANCHEZ

8 LETTERS
ANDERSON
GONZALEZ
MARTINEZ
ROBINSON
THOMPSON
WILLIAMS

9 LETTERS
HERNANDEZ
RODRIGUEZ

WALKER

MILLER

BROWN

♟ Hidden Pieces ♟
STICK AROUND

Can you find these **11 jigsaw pieces** in this photo of gumballs?

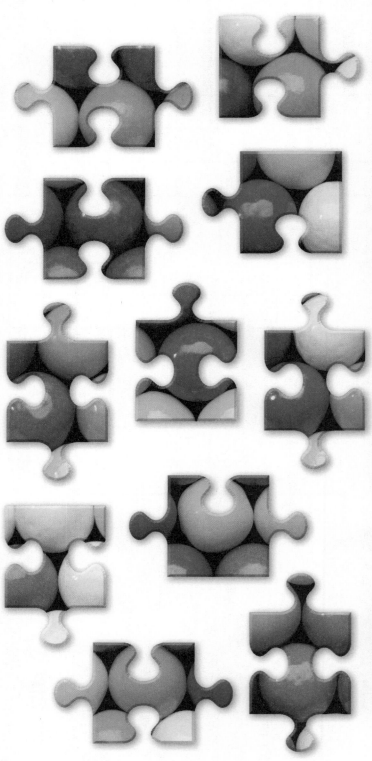

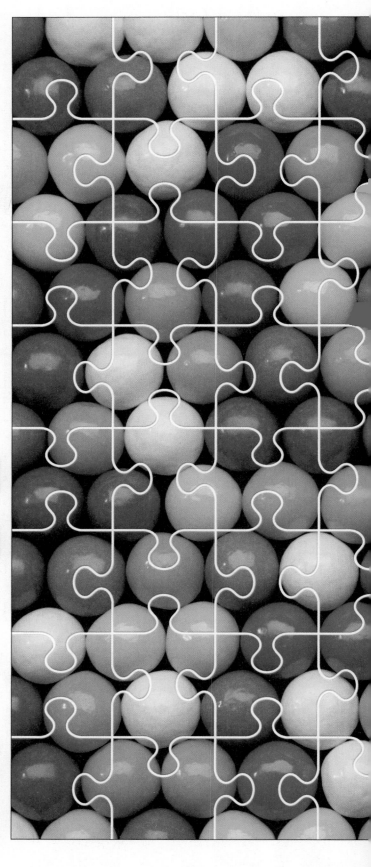

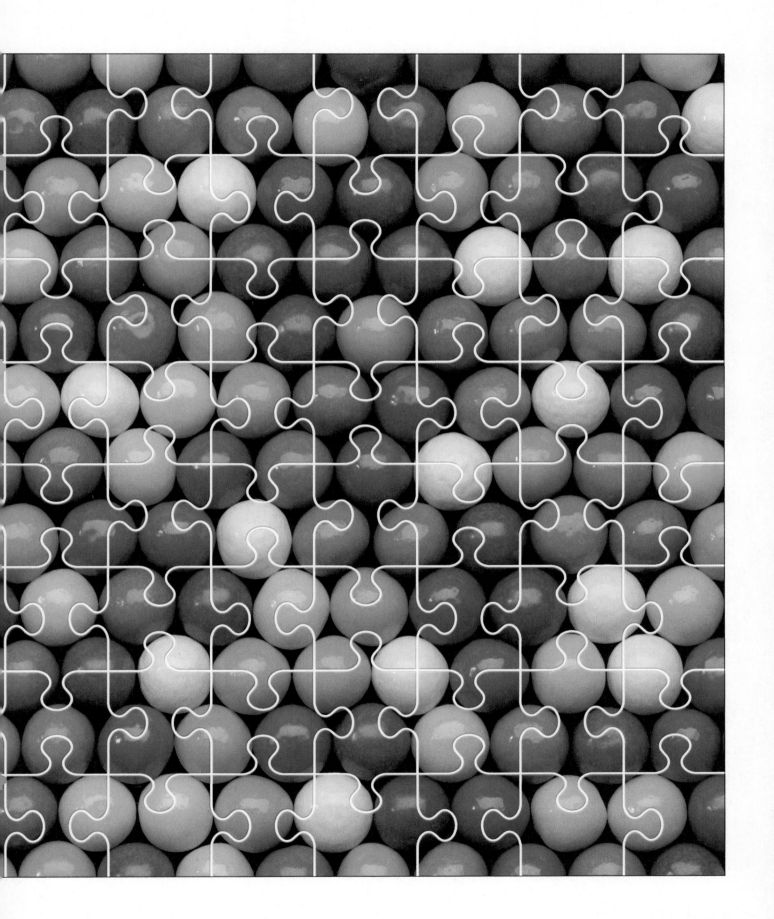

Each of these scenes contains 12 hidden objects, which are listed at the right. Find each object in one of the scenes, then cross it off the list.

Hidden Pictures® TAKE TWO

banana
bell
bird
boomerang
candy cane

drum
drumstick
envelope
fishhook
fried egg

game piece
ice-cream cone
ice-cream bar
lollipop
magnet

oven mitt
peanut
sailboat
screwdriver
skateboard

slice of pizza
snake
tooth
toothbrush

NUMBER CRUNCH

People, you know how to add, subtract, multiply, and divide, right? Then you can play calcudoku! Now give me 30 push-ups on the page. I said *NOW!*

HOW TO PLAY:

- To complete a game, each number will appear only once in a row and only once in a column, like in sudoku.

- The set of squares inside the heavy lines is called a cage. Each cage shows a bold number and a math sign. The math sign (+, -, x, /) tells you to add, subtract, multiply, or divide.

- The cage's bold number is the answer to the equation. For example, "12x" means that the numbers in the cage's squares must equal 12 when they are multiplied.

HERE'S AN EXAMPLE:

The only possible numbers for **2/** in this puzzle are 2 and 1. You may not know which number goes where, so write the numbers down as possibilities in the corners of the squares.

It's good to start with the multiplication cages. **18x** can only be 3x3x2. And just like in sudoku, you can't put the 3s in the same row or column (but they can be in the same cage).

An equal sign after a number means that you should put that number in the square.

Since the **2/** cage uses the numbers 2 and 1, the top square of the **4+** cage must be a 3.

The order of the numbers in a cage doesn't matter, but there's only one order that works in the finished puzzle.

2/ 1	2	4+ 3
18x 2	3	1
3	1- 1	2

CUTE 3x3 PUZZLE
(NUMBERS 1–3)

2-	2/	
	6x	5+

FRIENDLY 4x4 PUZZLE
(NUMBERS 1–4)

2-		6+	
6+			4=
1=	9+		
8x		3/	

FIERCE 5x5 PUZZLE
(NUMBERS 1–5)

25x		1-	6x	
6+			2=	10+
	7+			
	3=	4-	60x	
8x				

HINKS PINKS

Read each clue below. The answers are Hinks Pinks, pairs of words that rhyme. We did one to get you started.

HINK PINK:
Each answer is a pair of one-syllable rhyming words.

1. Bird grimace:
   __OWL__   __SCOWL__

2. Leftover seat:
   _____ _____

HINKY PINKY:
Each answer is a pair of two-syllable rhyming words.

3. Nicer pullover: _____ _____

4. Pet caretaker: _____ _____

HINKETY PINKETY:
The answer is a pair of three-syllable rhyming words.

5. Happier dog:
   _____ _____

BONUS ROUND:

1. **Hink Pink:** Runaway honker:
   _____ _____

2. **Hinky Pinky:** Meaner earring maker:
   _____ _____

3. **Hinkety Pinkety:** Pasta streamers:
   _____ _____

Round and Round

Use the clues below to fill in the boxes of this spiral—but there's a twist: the last letter of each word is also the first letter of the next word. Use the linking letters to help you spin all the way to the center. We did the first one for you.

1. One way to serve fried eggs
11. People eat these by the stack.
18. Fresh-_____ orange juice
25. Small, sweet fried cake, usually with a hole in the center
32. Machine used to heat slices of bread
38. Dried fruit topping for oatmeal
44. Popular flavor of jelly
53. Color of butter
58. Type of bread that is dark colored
67. This pouch sits in a mug of hot water to make a common breakfast drink.
72. What you pour over biscuits
76. Yellow parts of eggs
80. What you pour over waffles
84. Containers of yogurt are made of this.
90. _____ cheese is typically spread on a bagel.
94. Liquid poured over cereal
97. Utensil used to spread butter or jelly

 ART BY SARA VARON

WRITTEN BY CARMEN MORAIS; PHOTO BY LAURI PATTERSON/ISTOCK

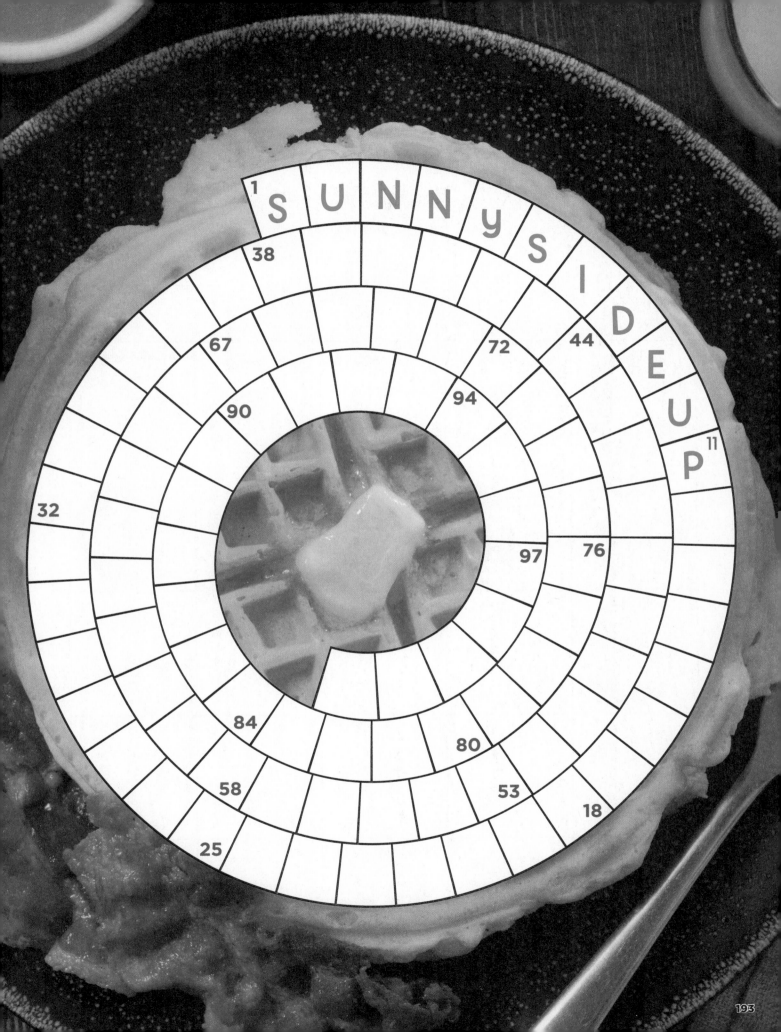

SUNNY SIDE UP

38 67 90 72 94 44 32 97 76 84 80 58 53 18 25

193

Food for Thought

CHEESE AND CRACKERS

Circle sets of four squares together that have two slices of cheese and two crackers. You are done when all the squares are in a set.

- Each set must have two cheese squares and two cracker squares.
- One side of each square must touch a side of another square to be in the same set.

Can you make all the sets? We did one to get you started.

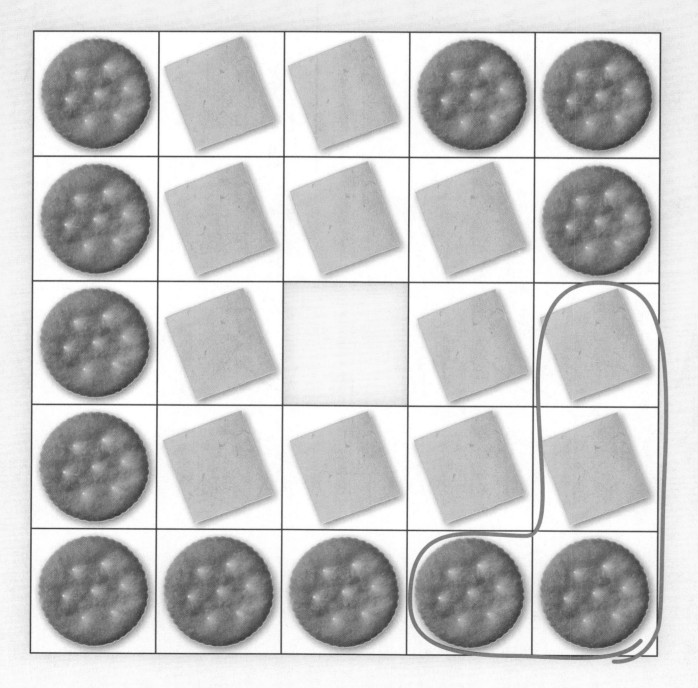

USE YOUR NOODLE

There are many kinds of pasta, and their names are Italian words that describe the pasta's shapes. Match each pasta picture to its name. We did the first one for you.

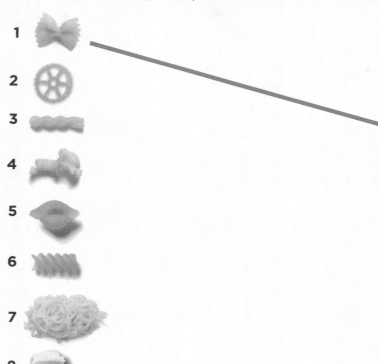

1
2
3
4
5
6
7
8
9
10

A. Campanelle means "bells."

B. Conchiglie means "conch shells."

C. Farfalle means "butterflies."

D. Fettuccine means "ribbon" or "tape."

E. Gemelli means "twins."

F. Orecchiette means "little ears."

G. Radiatori means "radiators."

H. Rotelle means "little wheels."

I. Rotini means "spirals" or "twists."

J. Spaghetti means "thin strings" or "little twine."

MIND YOUR MANNERS

Three of these facts about table manners are true. One is false. Which one is not a fact?

1. In ancient China, knives were used as kitchen utensils. But Confucius, the ancient Chinese philosopher, wrote that "honorable men" should not allow knives at their table. Chopsticks became the only utensil for eating in that country.

2. In Australia during the 1800s, it was considered polite to sneeze a few times after a meal to show appreciation for the food.

3. In the early days of the American colonies, Pilgrim children stood at the table during mealtime to show respect for their elders.

4. George Washington wrote a guide to good behavior when he was 16 years old. One of his tips was: "Cleanse not your teeth with the tablecloth."

Take a DIP

Hot summer afternoons bring crowds to the town pool. Can you find **12 objects or actions** that rhyme with *DIP*?

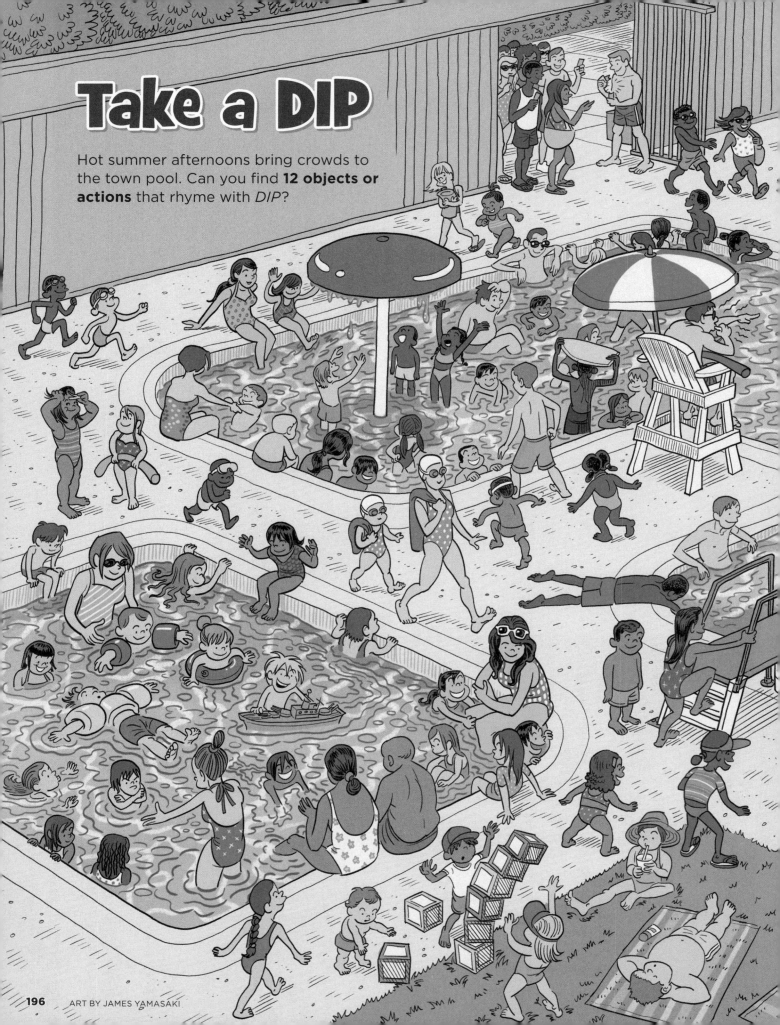

ART BY JAMES YAMASAKI

Class Trek: Quarkle Middle School Visits Earth

D-Leader and the students in her out-of-this-world cultures class are on another field trip. This time, they left Planet Q to visit the Great Wall of China. As usual, all the students got lost in a flash. Can you help D-Leader find her **6 students** in the big scene? Then look for the items on their field-trip checklist. Check off each one you find.

Can you find my students in the crowd?

J-KUB   B-BOP   KAY-T   C-YAH   N-DROO   BUG-Z

FIELD-TRIP CHECKLIST

- [ ] 2 yellow hats
- [ ] 1 orange backpack
- [ ] 3 birds
- [ ] 3 maps
- [ ] 5 water bottles
- [ ] 7 cell phones
- [ ] 1 polka-dotted scarf
- [ ] 1 green purse
- [ ] 1 pair of binoculars
- [ ] 1 baby stroller
- [ ] 1 red baseball cap
- [ ] 1 pink balloon
- [ ] 1 harmonica
- [ ] 4 umbrellas
- [ ] 1 superhero cape
- [ ] 1 lollipop

ART BY CHUCK DILLON

On a Roll

Every Sunday afternoon is game day on Oak Street. Join the fun, and see if you can find the **20 hidden objects**.

arrow

artist's brush

bell

boomerang

button

cherries

crocodile

eggplant

envelope

feather

glove

horseshoe

ladder

paper clip

pencil

screwdriver

slice of pizza

spoon

tea bag

toothbrush

BONUS GOAL: Can you find 5 squirrels in this scene?

ART BY IRYNA BODNARUK

The Legion OF Super Solvers™

This super trio (from left, the Gentleman Gorilla™, Count Yoga™, and the Human Turnip™) uses puzzle powers to keep the world safe from wrong answers.

THE CASE OF THE COOKED TROPHIES

The villain society PFFT—Puzzle Fiends Fighting Together—has struck inside the Super Solvers' headquarters. A supervillain took the Super Solvers' puzzle trophies and hid them in a giant, homemade lasagna! The thief left behind three puzzles that will reveal her name. Can you solve them and capture the crooked cook?

Each puzzle will give you a key word. Use all three key words to catch the evil supervillain.

Watch Your Step!

The mystery villain left specific instructions for this puzzle. Follow the directions to discover the key word.

Step 1. If the names of four months start with a vowel, write A; otherwise, write B: ___

Step 2. If the sun rises in the east, write E. If it rises in the west, write W: ___

Step 3. If you find a a repeated word in this sentence, write it down: ___

Step 4. If this sentence has over seventeen words, write the fifth letter of the seventh word; otherwise, leave the blank empty: ___

Step 5. If you add a letter to the beginning of the word APE, you'll make the name of something sticky. Write down the letter: ___

Step 6. If Millard Fillmore was a United States president, write S; otherwise, write W: ___

Step 7. If there are no missmelled words in this sentence, write the letters LY; otherwize, leave the blank empty: ___

Step 8. If 9 x 8 equals an odd number, cross out your answers in the odd-numbered steps. If it's an even number, cross out your answers in the even-numbered steps.

Write the remaining letters.

KEY WORD: _____ _____ _____

EGAD! MY HAIRIEST-PUZZLE-CHAMP TROPHY IS ENROBED IN *TOMATO SAUCE.* IT'S TIME TO COOK THIS FIEND'S *GOOSE!*

The Gentleman Gorilla

202

Count Yoga

Mozzarella Maze

The villain covered Count Yoga's Best-Solving-While-Stretching trophy with cheese and placed it in the center of this maze. Find the only path from START to FINISH. Then write down the letters you passed through in order. That's your key word.

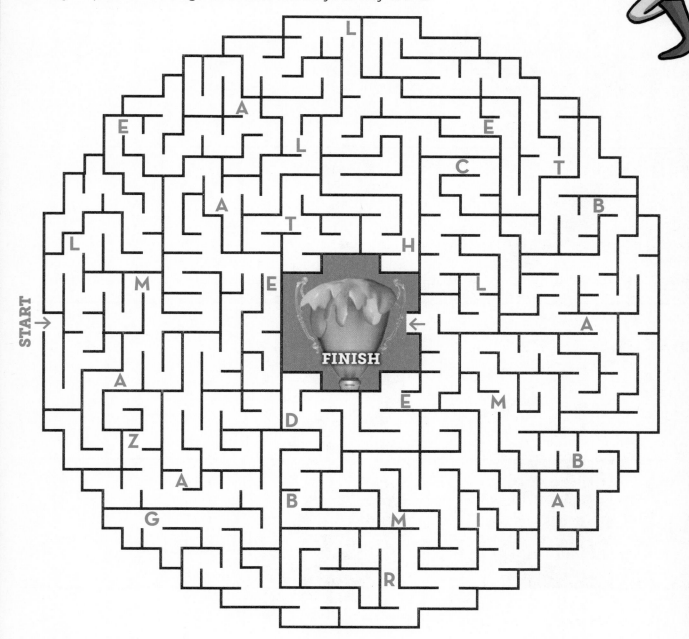

Write the letters you passed through in order.

KEY WORD: _____ _____ _____ _____ _____ _____ _____ _____ _____

WRITTEN BY ANDREW BRISMAN; ART BY R. SIKORYAK; PHOTOS BY BRAND X PICTURES/EXACTOSTOCK-1555/SUPERSTOCK (CHEESE); RUBBERBALL/SUPERSTOCK (TROPHY)

Take It Away

Each math problem below has two pictured words that contain the same letters except for one. Do the subtraction to find your key word.

MY MIGHTY-VEGETABLE-PUZZLER AWARD DOES *NOT* GO WELL WITH PASTA. I'M GOING TO GET TO THE *ROOT* OF THIS CRIME.

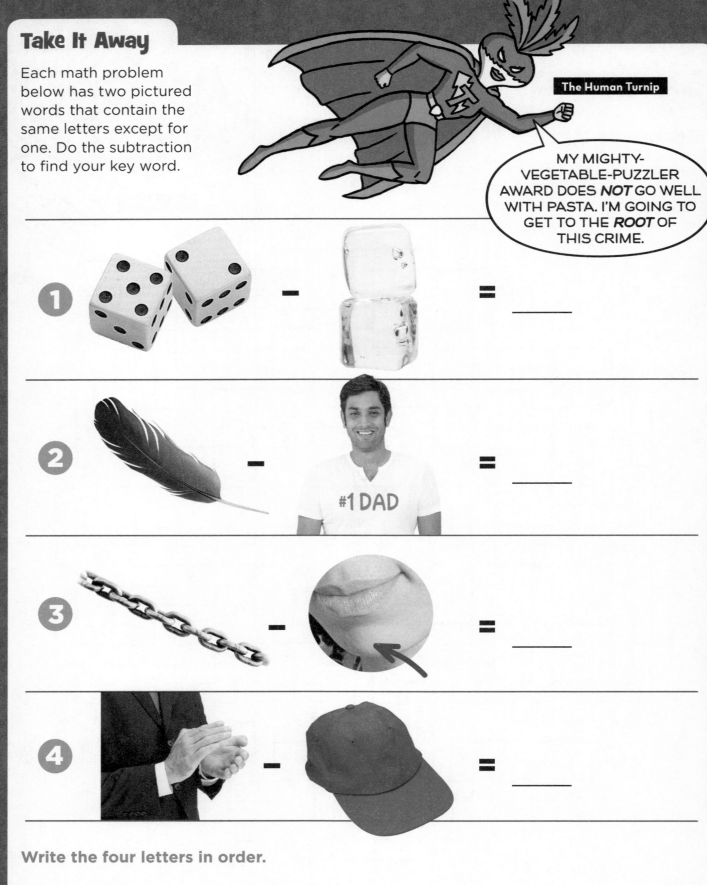

1 ⬜ - ⬜ = ____

2 ⬜ - ⬜ = ____

3 ⬜ - ⬜ = ____

4 ⬜ - ⬜ = ____

Write the four letters in order.

KEY WORD: ____ ____ ____ ____

PHOTOS BY JULES FRAZIER/EXACTOSTOCK/SUPERSTOCK (DICE); VINCENZO LOMBARDO/EXACTOSTOCK/SUPERSTOCK (ICE CUBES); HANS NELEMAN/EXACTOSTOCK/SUPERSTOCK (FEATHER); MAX OPPENHEIM/EXACTOSTOCK/SUPERSTOCK (MAN IN T-SHIRT); FSTOP/SUPERSTOCK (CHAIN); BLEND IMAGES/SUPERSTOCK (CHIN); YURI ARCURS MEDIA/SUPERSTOCK (CLAPPING HANDS); C SQUARED STUDIOS/EXACTOSTOCK/SUPERSTOCK (BASEBALL CAP)

The Mystery Villain Revealed!

Place the key words in the blanks. Then copy each letter to the same numbered square below to catch the villain.

THE GENTLEMAN GORILLA'S KEY WORD:

___ ___ ___
10 2   9

COUNT YOGA'S KEY WORD:

___ ___ ___ ___ ___ ___
5 11   1   6   8 13

THE HUMAN TURNIP'S KEY WORD:

___ ___ ___ ___
3   7   4 12

THE VILLAIN IS:

1	2	3	4	5		6	7	8	9	10	11	12	13

> Well done! It's time to throw the cookbook at this half-baked villain. Now that you know her name, draw what she looks like here.

CAPTURED!

Hidden Pictures® PHOTO

FLAMINGO FRIENDS

There is more than meets the eye in this photo. Focus in, and see if you can find all **17 objects** hiding here.

 candle

 open book

 cupcake

 peanut

 football

 pencil

 heart

 shoe

 horseshoe

 slice of pizza

 ice-cream cone

 spoon

 ladder

 toothbrush

 megaphone

 wishbone

 needle

Food Court Frenzy

Grab a table and then find at least **25 differences** between these two pictures.

Can you find these details in the picture below?

Sizzling Summer Crisscross

Ah, summer . . . the perfect time to do a cool crisscross in the shade. The list below has 29 ways to have fun—some new and some classic—in the summer. They fit in the grid in only one way. Use the number of letters in each word as a clue to where it might fit. We gave you one to get started.

4 LETTERS

PARK

POOL

5 LETTERS

BOATS

KITES

WAVES

6 LETTERS

HIKING

7 LETTERS

CAMPING

FISHING

ICE POPS

PICNICS

TAG SALE

8 LETTERS

BARBECUE

BASEBALL

BICYCLES

LEMONADE

MINI GOLF

SWIMMING

VACATION

9 LETTERS

FIREWORKS

HOPSCOTCH

SEASHELLS

ZIPLINING

11 LETTERS

SANDCASTLES

WATER-SKIING

12 LETTERS

MARSHMALLOWS

ROCK CLIMBING

13 LETTERS

MERRY-GO-ROUNDS

ROLLER-SKATING

SLEEPAWAY CAMP

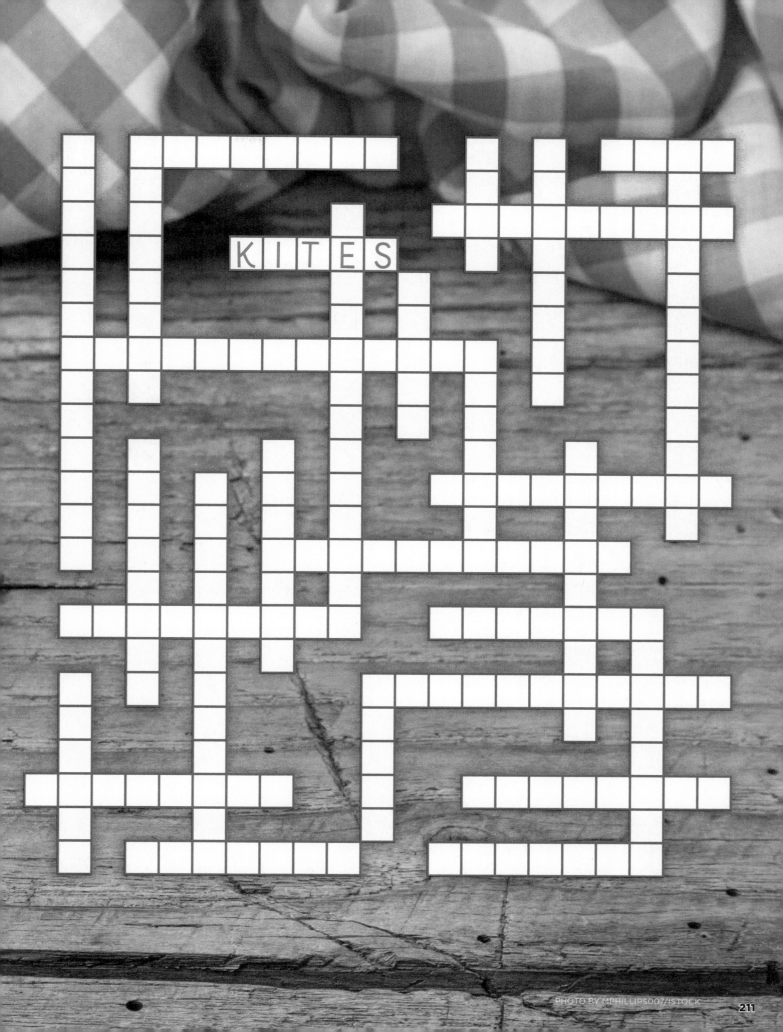

KITES

What's the Word?

Ten words have fallen to pieces—literally. Use the clues below to put the pieces back together. Each clue tells you the number of letters in that word. Cross the pieces off the list as you fill in the answers. Each piece can be used only once. We did one to get you started.

TIP: Some pieces may work for more than one word, but there's only one combination that forms all 10 words.

WORD PIECES

EAR	DAR	DOL	OME	TALO
~~POR~~	SI	DAN	~~INE~~	CATE
THE	THQU	~~CUP~~	BA	RW
GNAT	UPE	LAR	RY	DELI
ON	CAN	KE	AKE	
PHIN	LE	EN	URE	
LET	CAL	TTE	RPIL	

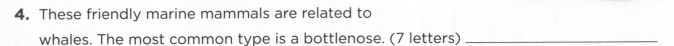

1. A small land animal with lots of quills (9 letters) <u>PORCUPINE</u>

2. A stovetop egg dish, often served for breakfast, filled with cheese or vegetables (6 letters) _____

3. A sweet melon that's orange on the inside (10 letters) _____

4. These friendly marine mammals are related to whales. The most common type is a bottlenose. (7 letters) _____

5. A sudden shaking of the ground that can cause a lot of destruction (10 letters) _____

6. Your own, "official" way of writing your name at the end of handwritten letters or on documents (9 letters) _____

7. A wormlike creature that turns into a butterfly (11 letters) _____

8. A common flower, also a weed, that starts out yellow and turns into a white puffball (9 letters) _____

9. This shows you dates, days of the week, and months, usually for one year. (8 letters) _____

10. A business that sells cookies, cakes, and bread (6 letters) _____

ANSWER THIS RIDDLE:

When you're done with the puzzle above, write the four unused pieces on the blanks to answer the riddle below. Start at the top and go from left to right.

What is at the end of a rainbow? _____ _____ _____

_____ _____ _____ _____ _____

Picture THIS

The words in each box show a common phrase. Pay attention to how the words are arranged to figure out the phrase. For example, in the first one, the word *JUST* is in the word *CASE*. So the answer is *JUST IN CASE*. Can you get them all?

1

CA*just*SE

ANSWER: JUST IN CASE

2

C U
the summer

ANSWER:

3

I'm you

ANSWER:

4

S   M
E   U
O   S
G   T

T   C
A   O
H   M
W   E

ANSWER:

5

HURR I CANE

ANSWER:

6

dishes

ANSWER:

BRAIN SQUEEZE

Use these tricky questions to stump your family and friends.

1 A truck driver is going the wrong way down a one-way street. He passes three police officers, but none of them stop the truck driver. Why not?

2 What gets wetter and wetter the more it dries?

Hidden Pictures®

6
by Six

Each of these small scenes contains **6 hidden objects** from the list below. Some objects are hidden in more than one scene. Can you find the 6 hidden objects in each scene?

HIDDEN OBJECT LIST

bell (4)	pencil (4)
carrot (3)	ring (3)
comb (3)	ruler (2)
crescent moon (4)	sailboat (3)
hockey stick (2)	screwdriver (3)
mushroom (2)	slice of pizza (3)

The numbers tell you how many times each object is hidden.

ART BY NEIL NUMBERMAN

Unidentified Sledding Object

Quick! Study this page for one minute. Then turn to page 218 to test your memory!

ART BY NEIL NUMBERMAN

Hidden in Plain Sight

Can you find the **12 piggy banks** hidden in this photo?

Did you study the scene on page 216? Now see if you can answer these questions. Circle your responses. No peeking!

1. What is the alien wearing?

   A SCARF   **A PARKA**
   MITTENS

2. What did the alien lose behind him?

   A MAP   **A HAT**   **A MITTEN**

3. What is the correct color of this girl's earmuffs?

4. What is the girl on the toboggan holding in her hand?

   A CANDY BAR   **A PHONE**
   A SNOWBALL

5. There's a puzzle piece hidden on page 216. Where is it?

   IN THE TREES   **ON THE SLED**
   IN THE SNOW

Where's the Cat?

Cats may have nine lives, but they also have 26 words in this puzzle. Circle the words containing *CAT* hidden in the grid. The word *CAT* has been replaced with a 🐱. Look up, down, across, backward, and diagonally. The uncircled letters answer the trivia question.

WORD LIST

BOBCAT	CATNIP	LOCATE
CATALOG	CATTAIL	MULTIPLICATION
CATAMARAN	CATTLE	SCATTERED
CATBIRD	CATWALK	TOMCAT
CATCHY	COMMUNICATE	VACATION
CATEGORY	COPYCAT	WILDCAT
CATERPILLAR	DECATHLON	
CATFISH	DEDICATE	
CATHEDRAL	DOGCATCHER	
CATNAP	EDUCATION	

D	O	G	🐱	C	H	E	R	C	A	🐱	M	Y
D	T	D	D	W	T	O	M	🐱	S	T	U	H
E	E	C	E	R	A	S	D	C	🐱	A	L	C
🐱	🐱	R	O	D	I	L	A	🐱	T	I	T	🐱
H	O	A	N	M	I	B	K	Y	E	L	I	N
L	L	L	A	W	M	🐱	🐱	P	R	T	P	E
O	T	L	R	A	P	U	E	O	E	S	L	E
N	🐱	I	A	🐱	T	A	N	C	D	T	I	D
E	F	P	M	E	S	🐱	N	I	🐱	W	🐱	U
P	I	R	A	G	B	E	E	🐱	🐱	T	I	🐱
I	S	E	🐱	O	🐱	A	L	O	G	E	O	I
N	H	🐱	B	R	N	V	A	🐱	I	O	N	O
🐱	E	S	S	Y	L	A	R	D	E	H	🐱	N

TRIVIA QUESTION:

What taste are cats unable to detect?

Put the uncircled letters in order on the blanks.

ANSWER: ___ ___ ___ ___

___ ___ ___ , ___ ___ ___ ___ ___

___ ___ ___ ___ ___ ___ ___ ___ ___.

Best Coaster Ever

Whee! Each of these **21 objects** has been hidden at this amusement park. Hold on tight and see if you can find each one.

 acorn

 banana

 bell

 carrot

 chef's hat

 firefighter's helmet

 fish

 fishhook

 flashlight

 horn

 ice-cream cone

 mitten

 paper clip

 pencil

 pennant

 ruler

 slice of bread

 slice of pizza

 sock

 teacup

 toothbrush

BONUS RIDE: Can you find 5 balloons in this scene?

Crossword in Space

ACROSS

1 Daylight source

4 Mars is called the _____ Planet

7 _____ Bang (theory of how the universe started)

10 *One* in Spanish or Italian

11 "A long, long time _____"

12 From _____ _____ Z (2 words)

13 ". . . then Snow White _____ into the apple."

14 Helium balloons are often made of this material

16 The Sun is this type of celestial body.

18 Venus or Mars, for example

21 "You can _____ your bottom dollar!"

23 Large container for liquid, usually with a spigot; a coffee _____

24 Continuously move around a star or planet

27 Halley's _____; heavenly streaker with a tail

29 _____ Grande

30 _____ Juan or _____ Quixote

31 The Milky Way is one

34 Destination for Apollo 11

38 Not outgoing; shy

40 "That's _____ small step for man . . ."

41 A chimpanzee or gorilla is one.

43 "Is that a yes or _____ _____?" (2 words)

44 Abbreviation for personal computers

45 Nickname for Theodore

46 Abbreviation for sergeant

47 "Get ready, get _____, go!"

DOWN

1 Long deli sandwiches

2 One _____ of measurement is an inch.

3 "_____ _____ chance!" (2 words)

4 Male sheep

5 Land of the pyramids

6 Toy baby

7 Ringling Bros. and _____ & Bailey Circus

8 "Tag, you're _____!"

9 Opposite of stop

15 Small battery size, but not the smallest

17 Abbreviation for a baseball statistic

19 It means *before* in poetry

20 Acronym for an explosive

22 "_____, phone home!"

24 Abbreviation for organization

25 Abbreviation for rich Internet application

26 Securely fastened; "I _____ the door."

27 Abbreviation for Denver's state

28 Letters between L and P, backward

30 "I really, really want to go to the party. I'm just _____ to go!"

32 Abbreviation for artificial intelligence

33 Shortened way to write Christmas

35 What you might say if you make a minor mistake

36 First word in a fairy tale

37 Cozy home for birds

39 Polka _____

41 All _____ once

42 Abbreviation for physical education

Explore new frontiers with the 10 clues about space in this puzzle. If you don't know the answer to a clue, look at the other clues that are around it, both across and down, or try another part of the puzzle and come back to the tough clue later. We did one for you.

1	2 U	3		4	5	6		7	8	9
10	N			11				12		
13	I			14		15				
16	T		17		18				19	20
			21	22			23			
24	25	26			27	28				
29				30						
31			32	33		34	35	36	37
		38			39		40			
41	42			43			44			
45				46			47			

WRITTEN BY BRENDAN EMMETT QUIGLEY. PHOTO BY CLAUDIOVENTRELLA/ISTOCK

WELCOME TO THE JUNGLE

There is more than meets the eye in this photo. Focus in, and see if you can find all **18 objects** hiding here.

 bell

 boot

 bowling pin

 butterfly

 comb

 dog bone

 doughnut

 fish

 heart

 needle

 open book

 owl

 sailboat

 saw

 slice of pie

 slice of pizza

 teacup

 toothbrush

Class Trek: Quarkle Middle School Visits Earth

D-Leader and the students in her out-of-this-world cultures class are on another field trip. They've left Planet Q to check out a concert at Millennium Park in Chicago. As usual, all the students got lost in a flash. Can you help D-Leader find her **6 students** in the big scene? Then look for the items on their field-trip checklist. Check off each one you find.

Can you find my students in the crowd?

J-KUB B-BOP KAY-T C-YAH N-DROO BUG-Z

FIELD-TRIP CHECKLIST

- 2 hot dogs
- 2 sleeping dogs
- 1 teddy bear
- 8 bottles of water
- 3 baseball caps worn backwards
- 2 blue coolers
- 3 slices of pizza
- 3 children on someone's shoulders
- 2 books
- 1 stroller
- 1 superhero cape
- 1 football
- 1 yellow blanket
- 2 bags of chips
- 2 slices of watermelon
- 1 wristwatch

ART BY CHUCK DILLON

Hidden Pictures®

6 by Six

Each of these small scenes contains **6 hidden objects** from the list below. Some objects are hidden in more than one scene. Can you find the 6 hidden objects in each scene?

HIDDEN OBJECT LIST

artist's brush **(3)**	mug **(2)**
canoe **(3)**	needle **(4)**
heart **(3)**	pencil **(4)**
ladder **(3)**	rolling pin **(4)**
lollipop **(3)**	snake **(2)**
mitten **(3)**	wedge of lemon **(2)**

The numbers tell you how many times each object is hidden.

ART BY NEIL NUMBERMAN

All Boxed In

Unbox this puzzle and you'll answer the trivia question below. Circle the 30 words or phrases containing *BOX* hidden in the grid. The word *BOX* has been replaced with ⬜. Look up, down, across, backward, and diagonally. The uncircled letters answer the trivia question below.

WORD LIST

BANDBOX	FIREBOX	SNUFFBOX
BEATBOX	GEARBOX	SOAPBOX
BOOM BOX	GIFT BOX	SQUAWK BOX
BOXCAR	ICEBOX	SQUEEZE-BOX
BOXES	JUKEBOX	STORAGE BOX
BOX OFFICE	KICKBOX	SWEATBOX
BOX SCORE	MATCHBOX	TINDERBOX
BOX SEAT	POSTBOX	TOOLBOX
BREADBOX	SALTBOX	
CASHBOX	SANDBOX	
CHATTERBOX	SHADOWBOX	

TRIVIA QUESTION:

In the 1800s, before cardboard boxes were invented, how were pizzas delivered? Put the uncircled letters in order on the blanks.

ANSWER:

Pizza was transported ___ ___   ___   ___ ___ ___ ___ ___ ___

___ ___ ___   ___ ___ ___   ___ ___ ___ ___ ___ ___ ___ .

K C H A T T E R ☐ I N A ☐
I S Q U A W K ☐ M O O B R
C ☐ D A E R B T M S C ☐ E
K E ☐ H S A C A O H R S D
☐ Z F F ☐ P T E N A P T N
T E I E F C R B E D O O I
A E R R H U A G R O ☐ R T
E U E ☐ A T N R O W I A S
W Q ☐ E K U J S C ☐ S G A
S S ☐ E C I N C S E I E L
S O A P ☐ O N T ☐ F A ☐ T
I ☐ O F F I C E T O O L ☐
S A N D ☐ N E ☐ T S O P R

WHAT A RIDE!

Feel the fresh powder as you search for the **16 hidden objects** in this scene.

- artist's brush
- banana
- baseball
- baseball cap
- candle
- eyeglasses
- frog
- funnel
- mitten
- paper clip
- pine tree
- shark
- slice of pie
- slice of pizza
- spoon
- train

Exit Strategy

You're at an amusement park with your family, and it's fun, except for all those totally terrifying rides. You don't want your little brother or, ahem, anyone else getting scared. Can you find a way out of the park without scaring yourself—um, scaring your little brother?

Entrance

HOW TO PLAY:

- Start at the ENTRANCE on page 234 and find the path to the SNACK SHACK without passing through any rides. Don't backtrack or repeat any routes.

- Once you've made it to the SNACK SHACK on page 234, go out through the SNACK SHACK's door on this page.

- Find the path to the EXIT without passing through any rides, backtracking, or repeating your route here, either.

5 State of Mind

1. Rhode Island
2. New Jersey
3. Louisiana
4. Florida
5. California
6. Texas

6–7 Sizzling Summer Maze

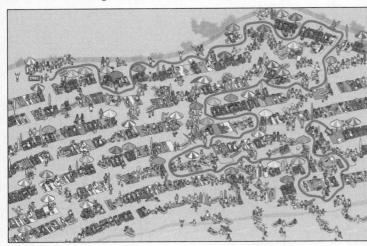

8–9 Chow Hounds

10–11 Brave New Crisscross

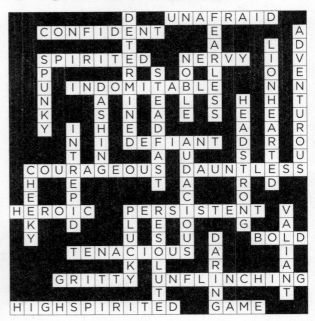

12–13 Monster Movie

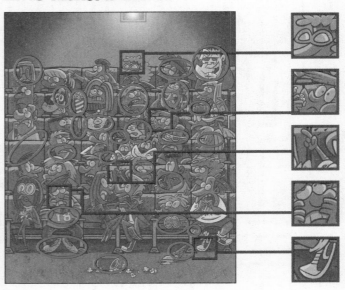

15 What's the Word?

1. VAMPIRE
2. SUNDAE
3. THERMOMETER
4. CONTINENT
5. TUXEDO
6. VOLCANO
7. SUBMARINE
8. BASKETBALL
9. ELEPHANT
10. BANANA

Joke Answer: If you leave alphabet soup on the stove unattended, it could SPELL DISASTER.

16 Test Your Memory

1. 1
2. Leash
3. Orange
4. 3
5. On a building

236

16-17 No Horsin' Around

Riddle Answer: HE WAS JUST A LITTLE HORSE.

18-19 Camping Out

20 Picture This

1. SWIMMING UNDERWATER
2. CORN ON THE COB
3. BROKEN HEART
4. ALL OVER THE PLACE
5. A PAIR OF PANTS
6. READ BETWEEN THE LINES

BRAIN SQUEEZE

1. Seven
2. His horse's name is Friday.

21 Hidden in Plain Sight

22-23 Let It Slide

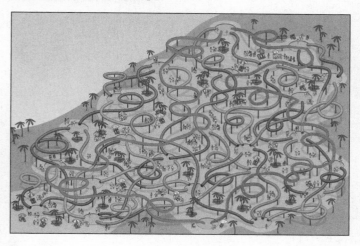

24 Hinks Pinks

1. Beach speech
2. Plain train
3. Colder boulder
4. Polar molar
5. President's residence

Bonus Round

1. Beef thief
2. Legal beagle
3. Vanilla gorilla

24-25 Go for a Spin

1. SLEDDING	60. COAT
8. GLOVES	63. TEETH
13. SNOWFLAKE	67. HEATS
21. ELVES	71. SNOWMAN
25. SCARF	77. NUMB
29. FREEZES	80. BLOW
35. SLUSH	83. WINTER
39. HOT COCOA	88. RINK
46. ANTARCTICA	91. KNITS
55. ARCTIC	95. SPRING

26-27 Zebra Zone

28-29 Keep on Truckin'

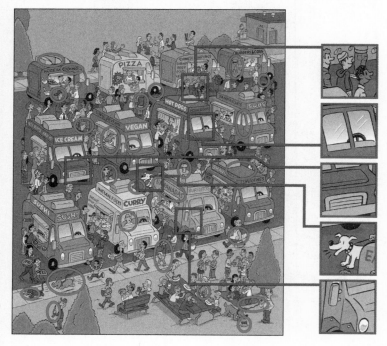

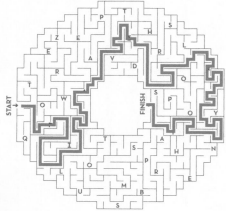

30-31 Up, Up, and Away!

32-35 The Legion of Super Solvers™

MOODY CLUES

The five words are *CRANKY, FURIOUS, GROUCHY, GRUMPY,* and *IRRITATED.*

The key word is **MUTANT.**

STOMPING GROUND

The key word is **PAINT.**

WEED IT AND REAP

1. *EYE, PIE,* and *TIE* rhyme with *FLY.*

2. *BEE* and *EGG* end in double letters.

3. *POT* and *TOP* have their letters in reverse order.

4. *EAR, ONE,* and *OWL* become *BEAR, BONE,* and *BOWL* when you place a *B* in front.

5. *CAN, PAW,* and *PEN* have one letter changed from *PAN.*

6. *HAT* and *HEN* become *WHAT* and *WHEN* when you place a *W* in front.

The key word is **CAR.**

THE MYSTERY VILLAIN REVEALED!

The villain is *CAPTAIN TANTRUM.*

36-37 For the Birds

38 Riddle Sudoku

B	A	Z	I	L	R
I	R	L	A	Z	B
Z	B	A	L	R	I
L	I	R	Z	B	A
A	L	B	R	I	Z
R	Z	I	B	A	L

O	Y	E	N	X	G
G	X	N	E	Y	O
N	G	Y	X	O	E
X	E	O	G	N	Y
Y	N	G	O	E	X
E	O	X	Y	G	N

Riddle Answer: BRAZIL

Riddle Answer: OXYGEN

42–43
6 by Six

39 Monster Pets

	Puff	Russ	Spike	Spot	Tiny	Ball	Bone	Flying Disk	Shoe	Stuffed Animal
Mom	X	X	O	X	X	X	X	O	X	X
Dad	O	X	X	X	X	X	X	X	O	X
Sister	X	O	X	X	X	O	X	X	X	X
Brother	X	X	X	O	X	X	X	X	X	O
Grand Fleezles	X	X	X	X	O	X	O	X	X	X
Ball	X	O	X	X	X					
Bone	X	X	X	X	O					
Flying Disk	X	X	O	X	X					
Shoe	O	X	X	X	X					
Stuffed Animal	X	X	X	O	X					

1. Mom throws a flying disk to Spike.
2. Dad throws a shoe to Puff.
3. Sister throws a ball to Russ.
4. Brother throws a stuffed animal to Spot.
5. The Grand Fleezles throw a bone to Tiny.

44–45 One Sweet Crisscross

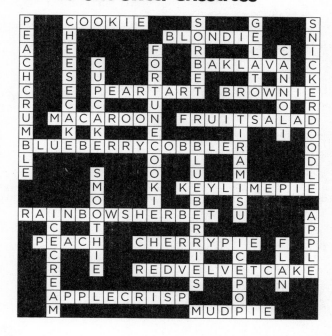

40–41 Class Trek: Boston

47 Dance Marathon

48 Test Your Memory

1. 2
2. Shovel
3. Blue
4. Five
5. On a scarf

48-49 Take the Bait

50-51 Match-Up: Dragons

Pair: 1, 5   Pair: 3, 9   Trio: 4, 7, 12

Pair: 2, 10   Pair: 6, 8   Single: 11

52-53 Carrot Craving

54-55 Number Crunch

CUTE 3X3 PUZZLE (NUMBERS 1-3)

3= 3	2x 1	6+ 2
1	2	3
1- 2	3	1

FRIENDLY 4X4 PUZZLE (NUMBERS 1-4)

10+ 2	4	6x 1	3
4	3/ 1	3	2
9x 3	2- 2	4	7+ 1
1	3	2	4

FIERCE 5X5 PUZZLE (NUMBERS 1-5)

14+ 5	4	2/ 1	2	11+ 3
2- 2	5	30x 3	4	1
4	9x 1	5	3	2- 2
1	3	2	25x 5	4
3	2/ 2	4	1	5

56-57 Class Trek: Paris

58-59 Squish Squash

60-61 Step Right Up!

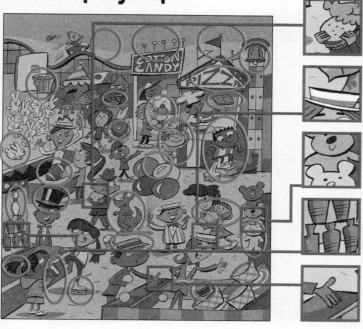

63 Hidden in Plain Sight

62 Monster Music School

	Drums	Guitar	Piano	Saxophone	Violin	Drakeula	Bruno From Mars	Lady GooGoo	Katy Scary	Three Directions
Mom	O	X	X	X	X	O	X	X	X	X
Dad	X	X	X	O	X	X	O	X	X	X
Sister	X	X	O	X	X	X	X	X	O	X
Brother	X	X	X	X	O	X	X	X	X	O
Grand Fleezles	X	O	X	X	X	X	X	O	X	X
Drakeula	O	X	X	X	X					
Bruno From Mars	X	X	X	O	X					
Lady GooGoo	X	O	X	X	X					
Katy Scary	X	X	O	X	X					
Three Directions	X	X	X	X	O					

1. Mom: Drums, Drakeula
2. Dad: Saxophone, Bruno From Mars
3. Sister: Piano, Katy Scary
4. Brother: Violin, Three Directions
5. Grand Fleezles: Guitar, Lady GooGoo

64-65 Rhymin' in the Rain

Brain

Cane

Chain (on bicycle)

Crane

Great Dane

Jane

Horse's mane

Maine

Pain or sprain

Plane

Spain

Stain

Train

Wayne

Weather vane

Windowpane

66 Just Add Words

(in alphabetical order)

+ sitter = BABYSITTER

back+ = BACKHAND

+ room = BEDROOM

blue + = BLUEFISH

+ worm = BOOKWORM

+ place = FIREPLACE

green + = GREENHOUSE

+ hole = KEYHOLE

+ mint = PEPPERMINT

pop + = POPCORN

scare + = SCARECROW

sun + = SUNFLOWER

sweet + = SWEETHEART

+ pick = TOOTHPICK

under + = UNDERDOG

67 Lights, Camera, Search!

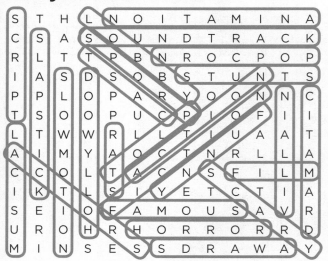

Trivia Answer: THAT POPULAR LETTER IS *E*.

68-69 Day and Night

70-71 Penguin Poses

72-73 Sit, Stay, Solve

74–77 The Legion of Super Solvers™

HIDDEN NATURE

The key word is **RHINO**.

TEDDY, SET, GO!

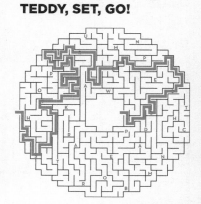

The key word is **STRESS**.

R U READY?

P + = PECAN   C + = SEESAW   D + = DEFENSE

O + = OCEAN   B + 4 = BEFORE   G + = GENIE

N + = ENTIRE   A + = ACORN   L + = ELBOW

The key word is **ENTIRE**.

THE MYSTERY VILLAIN REVEALED!
The villain is **THE SINISTER SNORER**.

80-81 Spot the Bad Bots

The bad bots are 2, 4, 6, 7, 9, and 10.

82-83 Under the Sea

84-85 Splash!

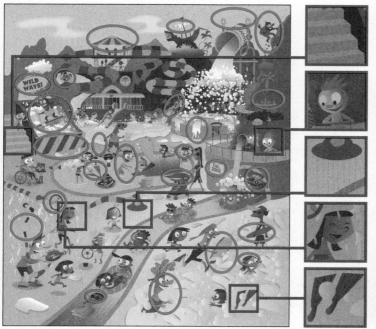

86-87 Number Crunch

CUTE 3x3 PUZZLE (NUMBERS 1–3)

3x 3	1- 1	2= 2
1	2	3/ 3
5+ 2	3	1

FRIENDLY 4x4 PUZZLE (NUMBERS 1–4)

3- 1	4	7+ 2	3= 3
6x 3	2	4	1
6+ 2	1	1- 3	4
4= 4	3	2/ 1	2

FIERCE 5x5 PUZZLE (NUMBERS 1–5)

64x 4	2- 3	5	2/ 1	2
2	4	4+ 1	3	5x 5
5= 5	2	12x 3	4	1
4- 1	5	4= 4	2	9+ 3
3/ 3	1	3- 2	5	4

88-89 Funny Business

1. OAR
2. BELT
3. NAIL
4. SOCK
5. YO-YO
6. APPLE
7. HEART
8. SPOON
9. GOLF CLUB
10. MUSHROOM
11. TOOTHBRUSH
12. BOWLING BALL
13. FOUR-LEAF CLOVER

What is the difference between a rabbit that runs three miles a day and a so-so comedian?
ONE IS A FIT BUNNY; THE OTHER IS A BIT FUNNY.

90-91 Merry Crisscross!

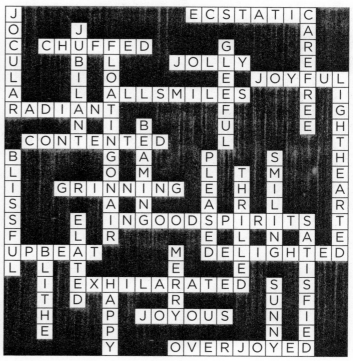

92-93 Class Trek: Rome

94-95 Flower Fun

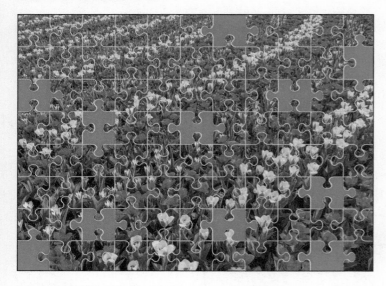

96-97 'Gator Skaters

98-99 Match-Up: Hot-Air Balloons

Pair: 1 and 4　　　　Pair: 9 and 12
Pair: 5 and 7　　　　Trio: 2, 3, and 11
Pair: 6 and 8　　　　Single: 10

100-101 Zebra Crossing

103 Picture This

1. MIND OVER MATTER
2. PUT IN MY TWO CENTS
3. MULTIPLE CHOICE
4. BROKEN PROMISE
5. HIGH CHAIR
6. TICKLED PINK

BRAIN SQUEEZE

1. The man was bald.
2. A mushroom

104 Test Your Memory

1. 7
2. Orange
3. Staying shut
4. Lobster
5. In purple coral

104-105 Where the ♥ Is

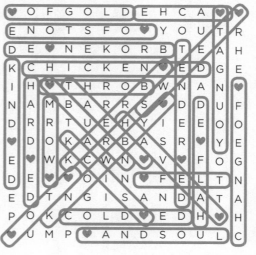

Trivia Answer:
YOUR HEART IS ONE GIANT PUMP.

106 Riddle Sudoku

T	L	P	S	I	U
I	U	S	T	L	P
U	I	L	P	S	T
P	S	T	I	U	L
S	T	U	L	P	I
L	P	I	U	T	S

Riddle Answer: TULIPS

S	A	H	U	Q	Y
U	Q	Y	H	A	S
A	H	U	S	Y	Q
Q	Y	S	A	H	U
H	U	Q	Y	S	A
Y	S	A	Q	U	H

Riddle Answer: SQUASH

107 Art Monsterpieces

	Headless Thinker	Moaner Lisa	The Screamer	Spooky Night	Whistling Mummy	1st place	2nd place	3rd place	4th place	5th place
Mom	X	O	X	X	X	X	O	X	X	X
Dad	X	X	O	X	X	X	X	X	X	O
Sister	X	X	X	X	O	X	X	X	O	X
Brother	O	X	X	X	X	X	X	O	X	X
Grand Fleezles	X	X	X	O	X	O	X	X	X	X
1st place	X	X	X	O	X					
2nd place	X	O	X	X	X					
3rd place	O	X	X	X	X					
4th place	X	X	X	X	O					
5th place	X	X	O	X	X					

Mom: *Moaner Lisa*, 2nd place
Dad: *The Screamer*, 5th place
Sister: *Whistling Mummy*, 4th place
Brother: *Headless Thinker*, 3rd place
Grand Fleezles: *Spooky Night*, 1st place

108-109 School Spirit

110-111 Peak Performance

112-113 Beware This Crisscross

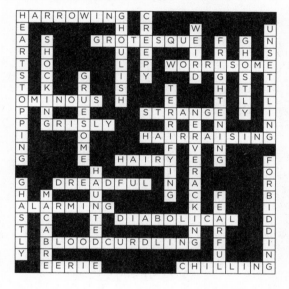

114-115 Freeze Frame

116-117
6 by Six

118 Hinks Pinks

1. Mouse spouse
2. Map rap
3. Stinky pinky
4. Turtle hurdle
5. Election selection

Bonus Round

1. Slick chick
2. Gruesome twosome
3. Manatee vanity

118-119 Going in Circles

1. CRIB
4. BLANKET
10. TUB
12. BEDROOM
18. MOON
21. NIGHT OWL
28. LULLABY
34. YAWN
37. NIGHTMARE
45. EYES

48. SHEEP
52. PILLOW
57. WAKE UP
62. PAJAMAS
68. SLIPPERS
75. STARS
79. SLEEPING BAG
89. GOOD
92. DREAMING

120-121 Bark and Park

5. CARROT
6. NEEDLE
7. TEACUP
8. ENVELOPE
9. GOLF CLUB
10. MEGAPHONE
11. TOOTHBRUSH
12. BUTTER KNIFE
13. HOCKEY STICK
14. CRESCENT MOON
15. SLICE OF PIZZA
16. PIECE OF POPCORN

1. BOOK
2. COMB
3. KITE
4. RULER

122-123 Party of Three

1. Farmer Fixing Fountain
2. Ducks Dressing Dolls
3. Elephant Eating Eggs
4. King Kissing Kangaroo
5. Hippo Heating Hamburger
6. Magician Making

   Meatballs
7. Goose Giving Gown
8. Lamb Lifting Lobster
9. Chef Carving (or Cutting) Cheese

124-125 Flock Together

126-127 Ready, Set, *SLOW!*

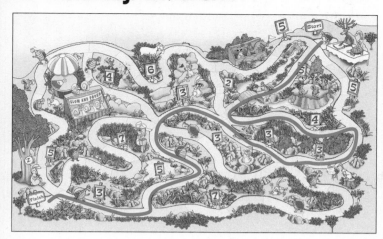

128-129 Spaced Out

130 Hidden in Plain Sight

131 In Orbit

1. Mercury
2. Mars
3. Venus
4. Earth
5. Neptune
6. Jupiter

132-133 Number Crunch

CUTE 3X3 PUZZLE (NUMBERS 1–3)

2x 1	2	9x 3
1- 2	3	1
3	3+ 1	2

FRIENDLY 4X4 PUZZLE (NUMBERS 1-4)

2x 2	1	6x 3	1- 4
1	4= 4	2	3
1- 4	5+ 3	1= 1	7+ 2
3	2	4	1

FIERCE 5X5 PUZZLE (NUMBERS 1-5)

10x 5	2	5+ 4	1	7+ 3
3- 1	5= 5	9x 3	20x 2	4
4	3	1	5	2
10+ 2	4	3- 5	3/ 3	1
3	1	2	9+ 4	5

134-135 Class Trek: San Francisco

136-137 Match-Up: Queens

Pair: 1 and 5

Pair: 2 and 3

Pair: 7 and 12

Pair: 8 and 10

Trio: 4, 9, and 11

Single: 6

139 Picture This

1. DROP IN THE BUCKET
2. FLAT BROKE
3. A ROUND OF APPLAUSE
4. SUDDEN DOWNPOUR
5. DOWN IN THE DUMPS
6. X MARKS THE SPOT

BRAIN SQUEEZE

1. No time at all. There is no such thing as half a hole. There's either a hole or no hole.
2. An anchor

140 Test Your Memory

1. 5
2. On icicles
3. Blue
4. Milkshake and tent
5. On an ice-cream cone

140-141 Splish, Splash, Search

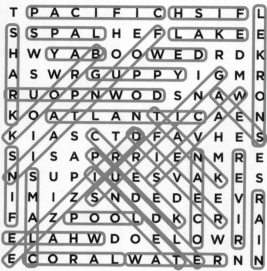

Trivia Answer: THE WORD *SWIMS* IS THE SAME UPSIDE DOWN.

142-143 Better LATE Than Never

1. Date
2. Crate or Freight
3. State
4. Grate
5. Rate
6. Skate
7. Bait
8. Eight
9. Inflate
10. Kate
11. Plate
12. Weight
13. Gate

144-145 Marching Madness

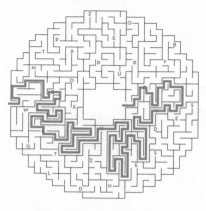

146-149 The Legion of Super Solvers™

SUPER SCRAMBLE

Count Yoga: CON, GUY, OAT
Gentleman Gorilla: LINGO, MANAGER, TELL
Human Turnip: HUMP, NUT, RAIN

The key word is **GEAR**.

THE BIG SIPPER

The key word is **BEHAVE**.

OH, SAY, CAN YOU SEE?

1. B: Nest; United States
2. E: Shoe; South Korea
3. G: Key; Turkey
4. H: Hand; Netherlands
5. D: King; United Kingdom
6. A: Fan; France
7. C: Comb; Colombia
8. I: Can; Canada

The key word is **TREE**.

THE MYSTERY HERO REVEALED!

The hero is **THE EAGER BEAVER**.

150-151 Mental Blocks

152-153 Hot and Cold

154-155 Such a Nice Crisscross

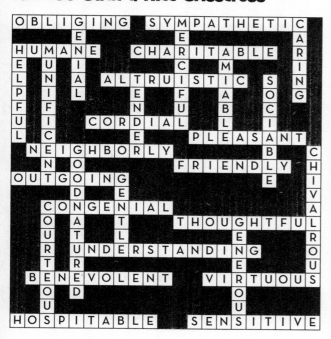

156-157 A Hop, a Skip, and a Jump

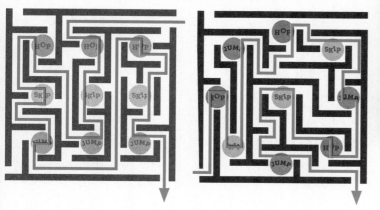

158 Fetch!

Based on average heights and weights:

1. Chihuahua: 6–9 inches tall; 2–6 pounds
2. Yorkshire Terrier: 9 inches tall; 5–7 pounds
3. Dachshund: 10–15 inches tall; 16–32 pounds
4. Border Collie: 18–21 inches tall; 30–49 pounds
5. Labrador Retriever: 22.5–24.5 inches tall; 75 pounds
6. Bernese Mountain Dog: 22–27.5 inches tall; 87–90 pounds

159 Body Language

1. GEYSER (EYE)
2. ARMY (ARM)
3. CHIP (HIP)
4. DREARY (EAR)
5. WHEELBARROW (ELBOW)
6. TOTE (TOE)
7. PLUNGER (LUNG)
8. ELEGANT (LEG)
9. HEATED (HEAD)
10. LINEBACKER (NECK)
11. QUARTERLY (ARTERY)
12. HAYWIRE (HAIR)
13. ASKING (SKIN)
14. BRAKING (BRAIN)
15. CRISPINESS (SPINE)
16. INTERESTING IDEAS (INTESTINES)
17. "STOP MARCHING!" (STOMACH)

160-161: Game Night

162-163 The BIG and SMALL Crossword

Crossword solution:

T	A	L	K				D	A	Y
A	G	A	I	N		T	O	N	E
N	E	W	T	O		P	O	E	T	S
		W	A	R	S				
O	C	T		P	A	S	S	E	D
L	I	E		S	P	Y		T	W	O
D	A	N	I	E	L		Y	E	T
	B	E	E	S					
O	F	T	E	N		H	O	W	L	S
F	O	O	T		Y	A	H	O	O
F	R	Y		T	O	W	N		

164-165 6 by Six

166-167 Match-Up: Cupcakes

Pair: 1 and 10   Pair: 3 and 6   Trio: 4, 7, and 8

Pair: 2 and 12   Pair: 5 and 9   Single: 11

168-169 Artist at Work

170 Riddle Sudoku

C	N	R	F	A	D
F	A	D	N	C	R
A	F	N	D	R	C
R	D	C	A	F	N
N	C	A	R	D	F
D	R	F	C	N	A

Riddle Answer: CANADA

D	N	R	C	I	E
E	I	C	R	D	N
I	C	N	E	R	D
R	D	E	N	C	I
N	R	D	I	E	C
C	E	I	D	N	R

Riddle Answer: DINNER

171 Fleezle Fitness

	Ballet for Beginners	Power Yoga	Strength and Tone	Super Cycling	Trampoline Aerobics	10:00 a.m.	10:15 a.m.	10:30 a.m.	10:45 a.m.	11:00 a.m.
Mom	X	X	O	X	X	X	O	X	X	X
Dad	O	X	X	X	X	X	X	X	O	X
Sister	X	X	X	X	O	X	X	O	X	X
Brother	X	X	X	O	X	O	X	X	X	X
Grand Fleezles	X	O	X	X	X	X	X	X	X	O
10:00 a.m.	X	X	X	O	X					
10:15 a.m.	X	X	O	X	X					
10:30 a.m.	X	X	X	X	O					
10:45 a.m.	O	X	X	X	X					
11:00 a.m.	X	O	X	X	X					

1. Mom: Strength and Tone, 10:15 a.m.
2. Dad: Ballet for Beginners, 10:45 a.m.
3. Sister: Trampoline, Aerobics, 10:30 a.m.
4. Brother: Super Cycling, 10:00 a.m.
5. Grand Fleezles: Power Yoga, 11:00 a.m.

173 Picture THIS

1. SLEEP ON IT
2. LONG UNDERWEAR
3. NOWHERE IN SIGHT
4. GO OVERBOARD
5. DOUBLE TAKE
6. ZIP UP

BRAIN SQUEEZE

1. Turn on one switch for five minutes. Then turn it off and turn on another switch. Go to the basement. The light that's on is the switch you just flipped. Feel the other two light bulbs. The warm bulb was the first switch you flipped, and the cold bulb belongs to the switch you didn't touch.

2. The word *short*

174 Test Your Memory

1. 1
2. Fish
3. Blue
4. 9
5. On the bus

174-175 Paws and Claws

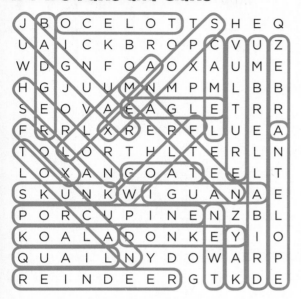

Trivia Answer: THE QUICK BROWN FOX JUMPS OVER THE LAZY DOG.

176 Hidden in Plain Sight

177 Stee-rike!

178-179 Pizza or Ice Cream?

180-181 Clown Food

1. KEY
2. BOOK
3. FLAG
4. ACORN
5. RULER
6. SNAKE
7. SPOON
8. CARROT
9. MITTEN
10. NEEDLE
11. FEATHER
12. ENVELOPE
13. TOOTHBRUSH

What do clowns like to eat for breakfast?
EGGS COOKED FUNNY-SIDE UP

182-183 Ride and Seek

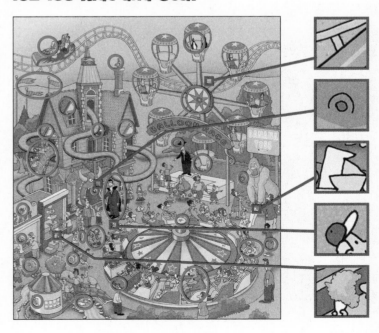

184-185 Name This Crisscross

186-187 Stick Around

188-189 Party Times

190-191 Number Crunch

CUTE 3X3 PUZZLE (NUMBERS 1-3)

2- 3	2/ 2	1
1	6x 3	5+ 2
2	1	3

FRIENDLY 4X4 PUZZLE (NUMBERS 1-4)

2- 3	1	6+ 4	2
6+ 2	3	1	4= 4
1= 1	9+ 4	2	3
8x 4	2	3/ 3	1

FIERCE 5X5 PUZZLE (NUMBERS 1-5)

25x 5	1	1- 4	6x 3	2
6+ 1	5	3	2= 2	10+ 4
3	7+ 4	2	1	5
2	3= 3	4- 5	60x 4	1
8x 4	2	1	5	3

192 Hinks Pinks

1. Owl scowl
2. Spare chair
3. Better sweater
4. Critter sitter
5. Merrier terrier

Bonus Round

1. Loose goose
2. Crueler jeweler
3. Spaghetti confetti

192-193 Round and Round

1. SUNNY-SIDE UP
11. PANCAKES
18. SQUEEZED
25. DOUGHNUT
32. TOASTER
38. RAISINS
44. STRAWBERRY
53. YELLOW
58. WHOLE WHEAT

67. TEA BAG
72. GRAVY
76. YOLKS
80. SYRUP
84. PLASTIC
90. CREAM
94. MILK
97. KNIFE

194-195 Food for Thought

CHEESE AND CRACKERS

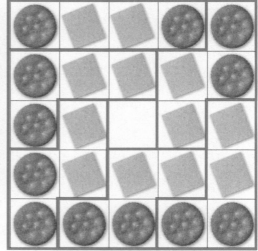

USE YOUR NOODLE

1. C	4. A	7. D	10. F
2. H	5. B	8. G	
3. E	6. I	9. J	

MIND YOUR MANNERS

Number 2 is false.

196-197 Take a DIP

1. Clip	5. Hip	9. Skip
2. Drip	6. Rip	10. Snip
3. Flip	7. Ship	11. Tip
4. Grip	8. Sip	12. Trip

198-199 Class Trek: Great Wall of China

200-201 On a Roll

202-205 The Legion of Super Solvers™

WATCH YOUR STEP!

Step 1. Three months start with a vowel (April, August, and October): B

Step 2. The sun rises in the east: E

Step 3. The word *a* is repeated in the sentence: A

Step 4. The sentence has 20 words. The fifth letter of the seventh word is S: S

Step 5. Add a T to APE to make TAPE: T

Step 6. Millard Fillmore was a United States president: S

Step 7. The words misspelled (*missmelled*) and otherwise (*otherwize*) are misspelled: leave the blank empty

Step 8. 9 x 8 = 72, an even number, so you cross out the even-numbered steps.

The key word is **BAT**.

MOZZARELLA MAZE

The key word is **MAMMAL**.

TAKE IT AWAY

1. DICE – ICE = **D**
2. FEATHER – FATHER = **E**
3. CHAIN – CHIN = **A**
4. CLAP – CAP = **L**

The key word is **DEAL**.

THE MYSTERY VILLAIN REVEALED!

The villain is **MADAM MEATBALL**.

206-207 Flamingo Friends

208-209 Food Court Frenzy

213 Picture This

1. JUST IN CASE
2. SEE YOU OVER THE SUMMER
3. I'M BIGGER THAN YOU
4. WHAT GOES UP MUST COME DOWN
5. EYE OF THE HURRICANE
6. DIRTY DISHES

BRAIN SQUEEZE

1. The truck driver was walking.
2. A towel

214-215 6 by Six

210-211 Sizzling Summer Crisscross

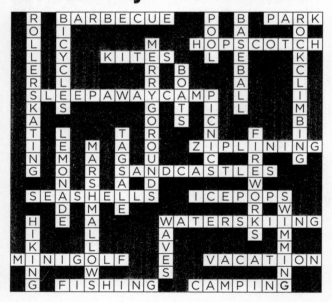

217 Hidden in Plain Sight

212 What's the Word?

1. PORCUPINE
2. OMELET
3. CANTALOUPE
4. DOLPHIN
5. EARTHQUAKE
6. SIGNATURE
7. CATERPILLAR
8. DANDELION
9. CALENDAR
10. BAKERY

Riddle Answer: THE LETTER *W*.

218 Test Your Memory

1. A SCARF
2. A HAT
3. PURPLE
4. A PHONE
5. ON THE SLED

218-219 Where's the Cat?

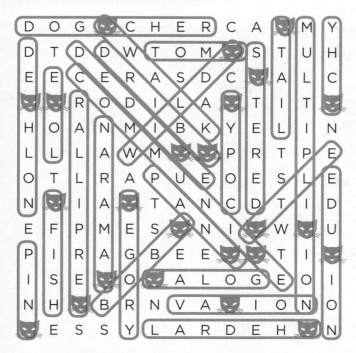

Trivia Answer: CATS CAN'T TASTE SWEETNESS.

220-221 Best Coaster Ever

222-223 Crossword in Space

224-225 Welcome to the Jungle

226-227 Class Trek: Chicago

228-229
6 by Six

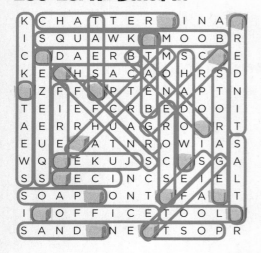

232-233 What a Ride!

230-231 All Boxed In

Trivia Answer:
Pizza was transported IN A COPPER OR A TIN CONTAINER.

234-235 Exit Strategy

For information about permission to reprint
selections from this book, please contact
permissions@highlights.com.

Published by Highlights Press
815 Church Street
Honesdale, Pennsylvania 18431
ISBN: 978-1-68437-261-4
Manufactured in Madison, WI, USA
Mfg. 10/2020

First edition
Visit our website at Highlights.com.
10 9 8 7 6